Go Native!

Conversation for English Language Learners

Myeong-Hee Seong
Katie Mae Klemsen

BAEKSAN
Publishing Co

C·o·n·t·e·n·t·s

SCOPE AND SEQUENCE

UNIT	TITLE	CONVERSATIONS	VOCABULARY	WHAT IN THE WORLD?	SITUATIONS
7	You Owe Me p89	Talk about items, prices, budgets, and expenses.	Budgets, store types and payment methods	The history of money	Go shopping, manage monthly expenses, ask prices and create a budget.
8	Time Flies When You're Having Fun p103	Talk about past experiences, personal facts	Expressions of time	Concept of time in different countries : Korea, US, Brazil	Discuss the past and ask about personal facts.
9	Five Years from Now p117	Talk about educational experiences, personal qualities, career goals	Career choices and benefits	Resumes in different countries	Search for a job, communicate work preferences, work experience and learn job interview skills.
10	Anything is Possible! p131	Talk about social issues, debate issues	Social issues	Global social issues over time	Communicate choices and debate social issues and topics.
11	Happy Trails! p145	Make travel arrangements, talk about destinations and documents	Travel and travel documents	Continents and countries	Make travel arrangements, talk about vacations and navigate international airports.
12	Wonderful World p157	Talk about facts, trivia and obligations and express expectations	Imports, exports and materials	Body language around the world	Discuss world facts and trivia, communi-cate global socio-economic dynamics and understand body language.
*	Appendix p171	Glossary of Common Idiomatic Expressions			

Unit 1

Friends Forever

Go Native!
Conversation
for English Language Learners

Unit 01 Friends Forever

Conversation

- Talk about old friends
- Talk about new friends

Situations

- Ask about past experiences
- Ask about present circumstances
- Meet new people
- Reunite with old friends

Vocabulary Preview

Friend	Colleague	Cohort	Classmate
Co-worker	Acquaintance	Age	Height
Weight	Hairstyle	Hair color	Nationality
Eye color	Interests	Last name	First name
Middle name	Nickname	Occupation	Ethnicity

Let's Get Started

1. Review this list of vocabulary words. Translate the English words into Korean.

▶ English	▶▶ Korean	▶ English	▶▶ Korean
friend		hair color	
colleague		nationality	
classmate		ethnicity	
co-worker		interest	
acquaintance		first name	
age		middle name	
height		last name	
weight		occupation	
language		cohort	
eye color		nickname	

NOTES:

2. Match the questions with the answers.

1) What's your name?	a. I am 33 years old.
2) Do you speak Korean?	b. I like to surf when I have free time.
3) How old are you?	c. No. I am a teacher now.
4) Do you still work at the bank?	d. My height is 68 inches.
5) What do you do for fun?	e. My name is Olivia.
6) Where are you from?	f. We attended the same middle school.
7) How tall are you?	g. I was born in California.
8) Didn't we go to school together?	h. No. In my country we speak English.

3. Pair Work. Use the questions and answers in part 2 to interview your partner.

NOTES:

4. Use the vocabulary words to complete Olivia Rose Mclaren's Internet profile.

Matchmaker Internet Dating Service

Profile

_____________ : Olivia
_____________ : Rose
_____________ : Mclaren
_____________ : 33 years old
_____________ : American
_____________ : Teacher
_____________ : 68 inches
_____________ : 136 pounds
_____________ : Surfing
_____________ : English
_____________ : Blonde
_____________ : Blue

5. Fill in the missing information for your own profile.

1) name : _____________
2) age : _____________
3) nationality : _____________
4) occupation : _____________
5) height : _____________
6) weight : _____________
7) interests : _____________
8) languages spoken : _____________
9) hair color : _____________
10) eye color : _____________

Metric vs. US Customary Units of Measurement

US Customary	Metric
1 pound	2.24 kilos
1 inch	2.54 centimeters
1 foot = 12 inches	1 meter
1 yard	1 meter

* Canada uses both the US and Metric systems, while the UK, Australia and New Zealand use the Metric system. Many Americans are also familiar with the metric system. Only the United States uses US Customary measurements.

NOTES:

Say It Right

1. Listen to the questions. Notice the rising or falling intonation.

   1) What's your name?
   2) Are you from Seoul?
   3) Do you have a brother?
   4) What color are your eyes?

2. Listen to the questions. Write ⇧ or ⇩ to indicate a rising or falling intonation.

   HINT Questions whose answers are YES or NO have rising intonation, while questions whose answers are not YES or NO have a falling intonation.

   1) What do you do? _____
   2) Are you a teacher in the United States? ____
   3) What color are your eyes? ____
   4) Do you have black hair? ____
   5) Are you very tall? ____
   6) Where are you from? ____

3. Pair work.

   Practice asking and answering the questions from part 2 with a partner.

4. Group work

   Introduce yourself to three classmates. Then ask questions about their occupations, interests, nationality, etc. Remember to use rising or falling intonations.

Speaking

Listen to the conversation between Olivia and Katie. Answer the following questions. Audio

Olivia : Katie? Katie, is that you?

Katie : Wow, Olivia. It's great to see you. It's really been a long time. What is it now, three years?

Olivia : Yes, I think so. It has already been three years since we graduated. Do you still work at the bank?

Katie : No. I haven't worked there since last January. I joined a new company.

Olivia : That sounds great, Katie.

Katie : What about you? What are you doing these days?

Olivia : Well, I have a new boyfriend. I think we might get married soon.

Katie : That's so exciting! What's he like? How tall is he? What color are his eyes? What about his hair?

Olivia : He's tall and has brown hair and blue eyes.

Katie : He sounds handsome. Good luck.

Olivia : Thanks, Katie. It really is nice to see you again. Would you like to have coffee with me?

Katie : I would love to but I can't. I have a yoga class that starts in 10 minutes. If I don't leave now I am going to be late.

Olivia : Oh! No problem. I'll call you this week. Do you still have the same number?

Katie : Of course. Some things never change.

1. Olivia and Katie are old friends. They have not seen each other in a few years. How do they know each other?

2. Pair work

   Practice the conversation with a partner.

3. Answer True or False for the statements about the conversation.

1) Olivia and Katie worked together three years ago.	T	F
2) Olivia has a new boyfriend.	T	F
3) Katie and Olivia went to school together.	T	F
4) Olivia recognized Katie first.	T	F
5) Katie and Olivia are angry at each other.	T	F
6) Olivia wants to drink wine with Katie.	T	F
7) Katie has a yoga class in 10 minutes.	T	F
8) Katie's boyfriend is tall and has blue eyes.	T	F
9) Olivia will call Katie this week.	T	F
10) Katie joined a new company last January.	T	F

NOTES:

4. Answer the following questions about Katie and Olivia's conversation.

1) What does Olivia's new boyfriend look like?

____

2) Where did Katie and Olivia meet?

____

3) Will Katie and Olivia drink coffee together?

____

4) Does Katie still work at the bank?

____

5. Fill in the missing words from the conversation.

Olivia: Katie? Katie, is that (1) ____?

Katie : Wow, Olivia. It's great to (2) ____ you. It's really (3) ____ a long time. What is it now, three (4) _____?

Olivia: Yes, I (5)_____ so. It has already been three years since we (6)_________ . Do you (7) _______ (8) ______ at the bank?

Katie : No. I haven't worked there (9) _____ last January. I joined a new company.

Olivia: That (10)______ great, Katie.

Katie : What about you? What are you doing (11) _____ days?

Olivia: Well, I (12)_____ a new boyfriend. I think we might get married soon.

Listening Comprehension

Listen to this short story. Listen for the main idea and details. Audio

Much has been said about how anti-social the Internet and mobile phones are. The truth is however, according to new research, communication technology is bringing people closer together. A study by the Pew Internet and American Life Project found family members were keeping in regular contact today more than ever before. And this is all down to e-mail, chat, our cell phones and SMS messaging. Years ago, it took a long time to write a letter, then find an envelope and go to the post office to buy a stamp and post it. Today, we write mail while we wait for our change in the convenience store and they're sent in an instant. Having free Internet telephone calls also helps us to stay in touch more often and for longer.

According to the Pew survey, technology has a very positive effect on communication within families. Researchers asked 2,252 adults whether new technologies had increased the quality of communication with their family. Fifty-three percent said it increased communication with family members they did not live with, two percent said technology decreased this. Numbers were similar for those living in the same house as their family. The project director Lee Rainey said: "There's a new kind of connectedness being built inside of families with these technologies". Survey co-author Barry Wellman agreed: "It used to be that husbands went off to work, wives went off to a different job or else stayed home... and the kids went off to school…and not until 5:30, 6 o'clock did they ever connect," he said.

1. Which title best fits the story? Circle your answer.

   1) E-Mail Makes Communication Difficult

   2) Research Shows E-Mail Improves Communication

   3) Families Suffer because of New Technologies

2. Answer the questions about the story.

   1) How is e-mail improving communication between family members?

   2) How many adults were asked about whether new technology increased or decreased the quality of communication with their families?

   3) Years ago, how did most people communicate with relatives that lived far away?

   4) What kinds of new technologies does this article mention?

   5) In your opinion, have new technologies improved your communication with family and friends?

3. Fill in the chart about how often you communicate and with whom.

Who?	How often?	How?	Why?
Best friend			
Parents			
Siblings			
Boyfriend / girlfriend			
Teacher			
Other :			

NOTES:

Food for Thought

1. Review these idiomatic expressions. What do you think they mean?

   1) Two peas in a pod
   2) We go way back
   3) As sweet as pie
   4) It runs in the family
   5) Blood is thicker than water
   6) Mum's the word

2. Pair work

   Discuss your thoughts about the definitions with a partner.

3. Match the expressions with the meanings.

1) Mum's the word	a. Be very similar
2) Two peas in a pod	b. Have common traits in many family members
3) Blood is thicker than water	c. It's a secret
4) As sweet as pie	d. Family is more important than friendships
5) We go way back	e. Refers to a kind and friendly person
6) It runs in the family	f. To have known someone for a long time

What in the World?

Listen to the recording about greetings around the world. Audio

The United States

When you visit the United States, there's no telling how you might be greeted. Common greetings include a handshake, a hug or a kiss on the cheek. Handshake hint: don't shake too hard and don't shake too softly. An overly firm handshake is not comfortable and a limp handshake can show signs of weakness.

France

A kiss, is a kiss, is a kiss... on the cheek that is. Two, three or four kisses, on the cheek, is the preferred greeting in France. Depending on the region, people kiss a different number of times. Kissing help: watch and learn. If you watch people greet one another on the street, you can learn how many kisses are common for the city you are visiting. This will help clear up any confusion.

New Zealand

The Maori, native to New Zealand, have a special greeting. They rub noses. Men and women rub noses together, as well as two women or two men greeting each other. Helpful hint: relax; it's not a romantic gesture. It's common between strangers, friends and family.

Japan

When people meet for the first time, they usually bow. In business, they also shake hands. In formal situations people might exchange business cards. It's polite to give and receive the card with both hands.

Special note: a smile can mean more than a smile in Japan. It usually means that a person is happy or thinks something is funny, but it can also mean that a person is embarrassed.

1. Pair work

Practice these greetings with a partner.

2. Group work

Are customs for greeting different in your country? Ask two classmates how they like to greet their friends, family and co-workers. Compare answers with a third classmate.

NOTES:

Unit 2

Campus Life & City Life

Go Native!
Conversation
for English Language Learners

Unit 02 Campus Life & City Life

Conversation

- Describe features of a campus, city, town
- Evaluate amenities
- Give reasons for likes /dislikes

Situations

- Make new friends on campus and talk about campus amenities
- Ask questions about the city, country and campus
- Talk about climate and location

Vocabulary Preview

Dorm	Laundry mat	Residence	Cafeteria
Meal plan	Subway station	Transfer point	Exit number
Downtown	Suburbs	Country	Wireless Internet
Climate	Location	Modern	Interesting
Safe	Quiet	Polluted	Historic
Crowded			

Let's Get Started

1. Review this list of vocabulary words. Translate the English words into Korean.

▸ English	▸▸ Korean	▸ English	▸▸ Korean
dorm		country	
location		wireless Internet	
laundry mat		climate	
cafeteria		crowded	
meal plan		modern	
subway station		interesting	
transfer point		safe	
exit number		quiet	
downtown		polluted	
suburbs		historic	

NOTES:

2. Match the questions with the answers.

1) Where will you wash your clothes?	a. It is modern and interesting.
2) Is your dorm safe at night?	b. No. I use wireless Internet.
3) Where do you have lunch everyday?	c. I like the country. It is safe and quiet.
4) What does your school look like?	d. I'll do it at the laundry mat.
5) Do you prefer the city or the country?	e. I eat in the cafeteria and use the meal plan.
6) Will you be in the library later?	f. Meet me at subway exit 6.
7) Where should I meet you?	g. No, I will be in my dorm.
8) Is this your internet cable?	h. Yes it is, but it is also crowded.

3. Pair Work. Use the questions and answers in part 2 to interview your partner.

4. How would you describe these places? Place a check (✔) in the box if you think the word describes the location.

What do you think?

	CITY	COUNTRY	CAMPUS
modern			
interesting			
safe			
quiet			
polluted			
crowded			
historic			

5. Fill in your favorite climate or location for the following places / events.

1) campus : ______________________

2) house : ______________________

3) vacation : ______________________

4) weekend trip : ______________________

5) job : ______________________

6) retirement : ______________________

7) swimming : ______________________

8) honeymoon : ______________________

Climates and Location

Climate is a word related to the weather.

- dry / wet
- hot / cool or cold
- tropical / arctic
- balmy or humid
- comfortable / uncomfortable

Location refers to the physical position of a place.

- central / remote
- quiet / noisy
- prime / undesirable
- busy

Say It Right

1. Listen to the questions. Notice the rising or falling intonation. Audio

   1) Do you live in the city?

   2) Which dorm do you live in?

   3) Do you prefer the city or the country?

   4) Where will you go on vacation?

2. Listen to the conversation between Lisa and Sean. Underline the words that are emphasized. Audio

   Lisa : You just moved from the country. What do you think of the city?

   Sean : It's great except for the bugs.

   Lisa : This is your first year of university. What is the best part so far?

   Sean : It's less stressful than high school.

3. Pair work.

   Practice each of the expressions in the conversation with a partner.

4. Group work

   Interview two classmates about their university and high school experiences. What do they like more? Remember to use expressions of evaluation in your answers.

Speaking

Listen to the conversation between Erin and Simon. Answer the following questions. Audio

Erin : Hi. My name is Erin. I am a freshman. Are you new here?

Simon : Yes, I am. My name is Simon. I live in this dorm.

Erin : Really? Me, too. I live on the 6th floor. Which floor do you live on?

Simon : I live on the 10th floor. Hey, I am on my way to the cafeteria. Would you like to join me?

Erin : Sure. I am starving.

Simon : Great. Let's go.

Erin : Simon, do you know anything about the meal plan?

Simon : Yea, sure. I have been using my meal card all week.

Erin : How do I use it?

Simon : Well, when you get hungry, go to the cafeteria and bring your card with you. Choose what you would like to eat and when you are ready to pay, you can hand the cashier your card instead of money. She will debit the amount from your card for you.

Erin : Wow! That is so easy. I thought it would be more difficult.

Simon : University is not so bad. I thought it would be more difficult, too.

Erin : Maybe we should wait until we go to class to decide if it is difficult or not.

Simon : You're probably right. Just wait for midterm exams.

1. How do they know each other?

2. Pair work

Practice the conversation with a partner.

3. Answer True or False for the statements about the conversation.

1)	Erin and Simon are new to university.	T	F
2)	Erin understands how the meal card works.	T	F
3)	Simon and Erin will study together.	T	F
4)	Simon and Erin live on the same floor.	T	F
5)	Erin lives with her parents.	T	F
6)	Simon spoke to Erin first.	T	F
7)	Simon has used the meal card all week.	T	F
8)	Erin is not hungry.	T	F
9)	Simon thinks university is not difficult.	T	F
10)	Midterm exams are this week.	T	F

4. Fill in the missing words from the conversation.

Erin : Simon, do you (1)______ anything about the meal plan?

Simon : Yea, (2)______. I have been (3)______ my meal card all week.

Erin : How do I use it?

Simon : Well, when you (4)______ hungry, go to the (5)______ and bring your card with you. (6)______what you would like to eat and when you are ready to pay, you can hand the cashier your card instead of money. She will (7)______the amount from your card for you.

Erin : Wow. That's (8)______ easy. I (9)______ it would be more difficult.

Simon : (10)______ is not so bad. I thought it would be more difficult, too.

Erin : Maybe we should wait until we go to class to (11)______ if it is difficult or not.

Simon : You're (12)______ right. Just wait for midterm exams.

NOTES:

Listening Comprehension

Listen to this short story. Listen for the main idea and details. Audio

The British government is soon to pass legislation that would raise the school leaving age to 18. The new plans will come into effect by 2013. Students will have the choice of staying in formal classroom education that covers academic lessons, or of receiving vocational training. It is the first major revision of the education age limit since 1972, when it went up to the present 16 years old. The government hopes the additional two years of schooling or training will improve the quality of young Britons and ensure more British youth have qualifications or workplace skills. If successful, Britain may be able to boast the best-educated and most highly trained graduates in the world. This should help the economy and it should also bring down levels of crime.

Britain's Minister for Education Alan Johnson told The Times newspaper that it was "disgusting that a youngster of 16 is not getting any training". He lamented on his mistakes of the past, saying: "I regret not staying on in education... when I left school there were many jobs you could walk into without qualifications. That's not going to be the case in the future." The leader of Britain's teaching union Steve Sinnott concurred. He described the upcoming legislation as "inevitable". He warned: "We cannot afford to neglect those young people who currently leave school at 16 unprepared for the rigors and demands of life in the 21st Century."

1. Which title best fits the story? Circle your answer.

    1) British Youth Leave School at 16

    2) Britain to Better Prepare Youth

    3) British Youth are the World's Best

2. Answer the questions about the story.

    1) What is the current age where British youth can leave school?

    2) Why is the government changing the age limit for leaving school?

    3) What benefits does this change bring to British society?

    4) When was the last time the British government raised the age limit to leave school?

    5) In your opinion, at what age should youth be able to leave school?

3. Finish these sentences with ideas and content from the story.

    1) The British government

    2) The Times newspaper

    3) Students are

Food for Thought

1. Review these idiomatic expressions. What do you think they mean?

   1) Go big or go home
   2) When the going gets tough, the tough get going
   3) Lose your mind
   4) Easy as pie
   5) Birds of a feather stick together
   6) Keep your eyes peeled

2. Pair work

   Discuss your thoughts about the definitions with a partner.

3. Match the expressions with the meanings.

1) Go big or go home	a. Think illogical or silly things
2) Keep your eyes peeled	b. When a situation is difficult, strong people work hard
3) Lose your mind	c. People who are alike do things together
4) Easy as pie	d. Watch closely, look for something
5) Birds of a feather stick together	e. Do everything or nothing
6) When the going gets tough, the tough get going	f. Very simple

What in the World?

Riding on a bus, in a subway or on an elevator is a common and rather essential way to navigate a city or university campus. Listen to the recording about subway, bus and elevator etiquette.

❶ Riding the subway in the United States is a little different than riding the subway in Korea. First of all, when you are waiting in line for the subway to arrive, you must stand to the side of the doors in order to allow passengers to get off first. Once the passengers have gotten off the subway, then you can get on. It's considered very rude to enter first. The same is true for riding the elevator. Let other people exit first, and then enter.

❷ Holding the door open for the person behind you while in a public place is an important cultural difference. In Korea, it's uncommon for someone to hold a door open for the next person. It is not rude to simply open the door and walk through. However, in many Western countries it is expected that the door be held open. A failure to do so is rude and disrespectful. Someone might even comment to you if you don't hold the door, especially if you are a man. The best thing to do is hold open the door with a smile. Doing something nice for a stranger can make you feel good.

1. Pair work

Take turns reading these passages with a partner.

2. Group work

Are customs different in your country? Ask two classmates their opinion of subway transportation in your country. Compare answers with a third classmate.

Unit 3

Just Like the Movies

Unit 03 Just Like the Movies

Conversation

- Discuss movies and celebrities
- Talk about music and musical icons
- Talk about stars and what they are famous for

Situations

- Go to concerts and movies
- Discuss pop culture

Vocabulary Preview

Romantic	Comedy	Chick-flick	Action
Drama	Horror	Science fiction / sci-fi	Fantasy
Cinema	Date	Fan	Celebrity
Agent	Famous	Icon	Concert
Classical	Rock	Rap / hip-hop	Country

Let's Get Started

1. Review this list of vocabulary words. Translate the English words into Korean.

English	Korean	English	Korean
romantic		fan	
comedy		celebrity	
chick-flick		agent	
action		famous	
drama		icon	
horror		concert	
science-fiction / sci-fi		classical	
fantasy		rock	
cinema		rap / hip-hop	
date		country	

2. Fill in the blanks with vocabulary words from part 1.

1) Traditional music is also called __________ music.

2) The Rolling Stones are a famous _________ band.

3) Madonna is a pop ________.

4) An _________ is a celebrity's manager.

5) A movie that women like more than men is commonly called a _____________.

3. Pair Work. Practice the sentences in part 2 to interview your partner.

4. What do you think of . . .? Write three related words for each vocabulary word.

1) Cinema

2) Celebrity

3) Fan

4) Country

5) Action

5. Use adverbs of frequency to write statements about how often you do the following activities.

Example : Watch movies : I never watch movies.

1) Go to the cinema :

2) Go to rock concerts :

3) See horror movies :

4) Listen to country music:

5) Go on dates :

Adverbs of Frequency

Adverb	Frequency in percentage
Always	100%
Usually	↓
Frequently	
Often	
Sometimes	50%
Occasionally	↓
Rarely	
Seldom	
Hardly ever	
Never	0%

NOTES:

Say It Right

1. Listen to the following questions about pop culture. Notice the stress and intonation of each question. Audio

   1) Are you a fan of Brad Pitt? _____

   2) What is your favorite genre of music?_____

   3) What did you think of the movie Slumdog Millionaire?_____

   4) Did you hear the latest news about celebrities and their agents?_____

   5) What do you think of classical music?_____

2. Listen again. This time, underline the words in each sentence that are emphasized. Do these questions have rising or falling intonation? Place an up arrow ⇧ or ⇩ a down arrow next to the question. Audio

3. Write three more questions about pop culture.

   1)

   2)

   3)

Talking about Pop Culture	Asking about Pop Culture
I think that...	What do you think about...?
I heard that...	Did you hear that...?
I feel that...	How do you feel about...?
I like...	Do you like...?
I dislike...	Do you dislike...?
My favorite...	What's your favorite...?

Speaking

Listen to the conversation between Monica and Penny. Answer the following questions. Audio

Monica: So, which movie do you want to see tonight?

Penny : I heard there was a new comedy out. Have you seen it yet?

Monica: No, I prefer action or drama. My life is more like a comedy. I go to the movies to escape. See what I mean?

Penny : Sure, but I don't like the fight scenes and chase sequences that drag on for hours. I always forget what the characters were fighting about.

Monica: Point well taken. Isn't there a chick-flick with that actress ...? Oh, what was her name?

Penny : Are you talking about Penelope Cruz?

Monica: Yea, that's her. It's a remake of an old movie from the 1950's. It should be good, or at least worth watching.

Penny : Sounds perfect to me. I heard the soundtrack to that movie was good, too.

Monica: I heard it was a mix of pop music created with classical instruments.

Penny : Well, let's see the movie, and then if we like the music, we can download the soundtrack when we get home.

Monica: Sounds like a plan. What time does the movie start?

Penny : It starts at 5:10. But you know, the first 20 minutes are previews, anyway.

Monica: Sure, but we had better hurry. We still want to get good seats.

Penny : All right, let's hustle. Traffic is always bad around this time.

1. What plans are they making?

2. Pair work

Practice the conversation with a partner.

3. Answer True or False for the statements about the conversation.

1) Penny likes action movies.	T	F
2) Penny and Monica want to see a concert.	T	F
3) They will see a chick-flick.	T	F
4) The movie starts at 6:10.	T	F
5) If they like the music, they will buy the CD.	T	F
6) The soundtrack is mostly classical music.	T	F
7) Monica's life is like a comedy movie.	T	F
8) Penny suggested a horror movie to Monica.	T	F
9) Penny doesn't like long action or fight scenes.	T	F
10) The movie is a remake of an older film.	T	F

4. Answer the following questions about the conversation.

1) Why doesn't Monica like comedy movies?

2) Why doesn't Penny like action or drama movies?

3) What information do you have about the movie Penny and Monica will see today?

4) What will the girls do if they like the music?

Listening Comprehension

Listen to this short story. Listen for the main idea and details. Audio

Models under the age of 16 will be banned from London's Fashion Week. In addition, all models will have to show a health certificate before they are allowed to walk down the catwalk. These are the decisions of the Model Health Inquiry that was set up in March by the British Fashion Council to ensure models eat healthily. One major concern was how skinny models have become. Super-thin is popular and experts fear that models are risking their health due to a variety of eating disorders. An unwanted side effect is that teenagers and young women in their twenties and thirties copy the looks and shape of size-zero models and put their health at risk. The inquiry is in response to the deaths of two Uruguayan models Luisel Ramos, 22, and her sister, Eliana, 18, who died last year because of poor diets.

The Model Health Inquiry did not recommend barring models based on their body mass index (BMI). It said that the BMI - the ratio of weight to height – was "not an accurate method of determining health". The inquiry said models could easily make themselves vomit to try and beat the tests and get on the catwalk. Other countries have barred models with a BMI of less than 18. The World Health Organization says a BMI of 18.5 is a minimum healthy standard. The report made 14 recommendations, which include random drug tests and a "rigorous scientific study" into the extent of eating disorders within the industry. The report also said that from September 2008, models "should provide a medical certificate attesting their good health from doctors with expertise in recognizing eating disorders."

1. Which title best fits the article? Circle your answer.

   1) Models Using More Drugs Now than Ever Before

   2) Models under 16 banned in London

   3) Models are Very Thin

2. Read the story out loud to your partner. Practice slowly and focus on your accent and pronunciation.

3. Answer the questions about the story.

   1) What is the minimum acceptable BMI stated by the World Health Organization?

   2) Starting in September of 2008, what will models have to do?

   3) Why are models at risk these days?

   4) How old will models have to be to participate in London's fashion week?

4. In your opinion

   Answer the following questions using your feelings, thoughts and ideas.

   1) Are ultra-thin models more attractive than other models?

   2) Are models risking too much for their jobs?

   3) What is a model's job? Why do they need to be so thin?

   4) Should models be famous for what they do?

   5) Do they contribute much to society?

Food for Thought

1. Review these idiomatic expressions. What do you think they mean?

   1) Just like the movies

   2) Steal the show

   3) Be a /the show-stopper

   4) In the limelight

   5) To make one's bed and lie in it

   6) To break a leg

2. Pair work

   Discuss your thoughts about the definitions with a partner.

3. Match the expressions with the meanings.

1) Just like the movies	a. Be very good
2) Show-stopper	b. Be the very best (out of many)
3) To make one's bed and lie in it	c. Have or attract a lot of attention
4) Steal the show	d. Good luck
5) In the limelight	e. Unreal or unbelievable
6) To break a leg	f. Create a bad situation and suffer the consequences

4. Group work

   Do you have similar idioms or expressions in your own language? Brainstorm in groups of three to four, about expressions of speech you use in your native language. Share your list with the class.

What in the World?

What's Your Sign?

1. Traditionally, Korean people use Chinese astrology, which refers to the birth year, while Western astrology is calculated by birth date. Western astrology is based on ancient omen readings from Mesopotamia. Use the chart below to determine your sign.

What do you think?

Sign	Birthdates	Characteristics
Aries	March 21 - April 20	brave, adventurous, impulsive
Taurus	April 21 - May 21	reliable, loyal, gentle
Gemini	May 22 - June 21	kind, generous, thoughtful
Cancer	June 22 - July 22	sensitive, artistic, excellent memory
Leo	July 23 - August 21	creative, generous, loving
Virgo	August 22 - September 23	methodical, diligent, quiet
Libra	September 24 - October 23	sensible, cheerful, charming
Scorpio	October 24 - November 22	intense, perceptive, secretive
Sagittarius	November 23 - December 22	impulsive, ambitious, optimistic
Capricorn	December 23 - January 20	ambitious, loyal, serious
Aquarius	January 21 - February 18	rude, practical, willing
Pisces	February 19 - March 20	positive, patient, gentle

2. Group work

Ask two classmates what their Western astrological sign is. Ask them if the characteristics are accurate for them. If not, what is different?

Unit 4

Epicureans

Unit 04 Epicureans

Conversation

- Talk about customs and habits
- Talk about food items
- Talk about the history of foods

Situations

- Eating on vacation and while traveling
- Discuss global food cultures
- Order specific food items at a restaurant

Vocabulary Preview

Chopsticks	Fork	Knife	Spoon
Toothpick	Bill	Ashtray	Salty
Spicy	Spoiled	Fresh	Poultry
Beef	Pork	Shellfish	Dairy
Protein	Carbohydrate	Dessert	Snack

Let's Get Started

1. Review this list of vocabulary words. Translate the English words into Korean.

▶ English	▶▶ Korean	▶ English	▶▶ Korean
chopsticks		fresh	
fork		poultry	
knife		beef	
spoon		pork	
toothpick		shellfish	
bill / check		dairy	
ashtray		protein	
salty		carbohydrate	
spicy		dessert	
spoiled		snack	

2. Write a sentence with the vocabulary words from part 1.

1) Salty :

2) Bill / Check :

3) Toothpick :

4) Chopsticks :

5) Snack :

3. Pair Work

Read your sentences from part 2 to your partner. Listen to their sentences.

4. Classify the words in the box below. Write the names of the food items beneath the correct category.

pork	bread	lobster	apricots	bean sprouts	cheese
yogurt	poultry	sausage	rice	clams	persimmons
coconuts	squid	chestnuts	figs	eggs	milk
mussels	fish	almonds	shrimp	beans	cucumbers

Food Groups and Categories

Protein		Carbohydrate
Shellfish	**Dairy**	**Fruit / Vegetable**

5. Group work

To find out if you were right, ask two classmates their answers. Compare classifications.

Say It Right

Listen to the following passages about food. Notice the stress and intonation of each sentence. Audio

❶ Fish can be eaten raw or cooked. Raw fish has been eaten in Japan for centuries. Japan has always fed its population from the sea and rice fields. Putting a slice of fish on top of a portion of rice was a logical and delicious idea.

❷ Potatoes were discovered in Peru and carried back to Europe in the 1500's by the Spanish explorers. Potatoes were eaten baked or boiled. Today, they are most commonly eaten fried and called French fries.

❸ The Chinese introduced a cooking style called sautéing to the Western world. Food is quickly cooked in oil or butter over high heat. It helps prevent vegetables from overcooking. It's healthier and more delicious than many other ways of cooking. When you sauté, the food maintains most of its nutrients.

❹ Many people say that spaghetti was invented in China and brought to Venice, Italy by Marco Polo. It is also possible that this food was invented in ancient Sicily. Either way, spaghetti is not an English word; it's Italian.

1. Listen again. This time, underline words that are stressed and emphasized by the speaker's voice.

2. Pair work

Practice each statement from part 1 with your partner.

Speaking

Listen to the conversation between Garrick and Charlotte. Answer the following questions. Audio

Garrick : Charlotte, what do you feel like having for lunch?

Charlotte : I'm up for anything, really. Do you like Chinese? They make really great sautéed spinach at the Happy Dragon downtown.

Garrick : I do, but I just had it for dinner. I don't want to eat too much greasy food. I'm watching the waistline, you know.

Charlotte : Okay, then, how about Japanese? You like sushi, don't you?

Garrick : I don't like the idea of raw fish. It's the texture, not the taste. I think of chewing it and all I can imagine is a piece of slimy meat.

Charlotte : Well, that leaves us with Mexican. Do you fancy a burrito?

Garrick : I wish I could say yes, but my old roommate was Mexican and all we ever ate was burrito after burrito after burrito...

Charlotte : I get your point : no Mexican. You're a little pickier than usual, so why don't you make a suggestion?

Garrick : I want something fresh and healthy. I prefer vegetables to meat, too. It's too hard to eat out these days. Everything is either fried or ... wait! I have an idea! Why don't you cook for us?

Charlotte : You want me to cook?

Garrick : Sure. Then we can have something tasty, spicy, fresh, whatever! We can have it just the way we like it.

Charlotte : Well, it sounds like a lot of work.

Garrick : Hey, if you cook, I'll clean.

Charlotte : It's a deal!

1. What ethnic foods are they considering to eat?

2. Pair work

Practice the conversation with a partner.

3. Answer True or False for the statements about the conversation.

1) Charlotte will cook for Garrick.	T	F
2) The Happy Dragon has fried spinach.	T	F
3) Garrick is on a diet.	T	F
4) Charlotte suggested sushi to Garrick.	T	F
5) Charlotte's former roommate was from Mexico.	T	F
6) Garrick is picky today.	T	F
7) Garrick will cook and Charlotte will clean.	T	F
8) Garrick wants something spicy.	T	F
9) Charlotte is up for anything.	T	F
10) Garrick likes raw fish.	T	F

4. Four phrases are underlined in the conversation. What do they mean? Write the answers below. Use context clues from the conversation for help.

1) <u>I'm up for anything</u>:

2) <u>Watching the waistline</u>:

3) <u>Fancy a burrito</u>:

4) <u>I get your point</u>:

Listening Comprehension

Listen to this short story. Listen for the main idea and details. Audio

What do you buy the man who has everything for Christmas? How about some perfume that smells of meat? The US hamburger giant Burger King has just released a fragrance for men based on the smell of its Whopper burger. The company is advertising the scent, called Flame, on its website firemeetsdesire.com. It says: "The Whopper sandwich is America's favorite burger. Flame captures the essence of that love and gives it to you." The website also invites visitors to "Behold the scent of seduction." The site features a variety of romantic images, including candlelit baths, wine and sunsets. Burger King says Flame will allow men to "Set the mood no matter what mood you're in the mood for".

The scent is on sale online for $3.99, although just five days before Christmas, it was sold out. It is on sale in New York, for those who desperately want to buy a bottle. The website that is marketing Flame has a lot of feedback from some very satisfied customers. It seems the body spray is doing some amazing things to make men more irresistible. We found several people who were more than happy with their purchase. Jason Lowe from San Diego said: "I like the smell but would like the body spray to have the smell of extra cheese." Carmen Diaz from Los Angeles said she loved the smell, but was worried about the number of dogs that now followed her husband. The fragrance has not yet been a big hit with vegetarians.

1. Which title best fits the article? Circle your answer.

   1) Meat Smells Nice

   2) Vegetarians Want to Smell Like Meat

   3) Burger King Creates a Meat Fragrance

2. Read the story out loud to your partner. Practice slowly and focus on your accent and pronunciation.

3. Pair work

   Which food smells do you like the best?

4. Mark true or false for the following statements about the story.

1) Burger King is selling perfume that smells like meat.	T	F
2) The new fragrance is called 'Fire, Meat, Desire'.	T	F
3) Burger King's Whopper is America's favorite burger.	T	F
4) There is plenty of the perfume left if you want to buy it online.	T	F
5) A man wore the scent and started following dogs.	T	F
6) The biggest customers for the perfume are vegetarians.	T	F

5. Match the synonyms from the story.

1) perfume	a. comments
2) captures	b. concerned
3) essence	c. presents

4) features d. success

5) mood e. fragrance

6) desperately f. core

7) feedback g. urgently

8) irresistible h. atmosphere

9) worried i. catches

10) big hit j. attractive

6. In your opinion ...

Would you wear a perfume that smelled like meat? What about another food? Check the scents that you would use as a perfume.

a. _____ meat

b. _____ apple pie

c. _____ grape

d. _____ coconut

e. _____ chonggukjang

f. _____ fish

NOTES:

Food for Thought

1. Review these idiomatic expressions. What do you think they mean?

   1) Food for thought
   2) Eat it up
   3) Couch potato
   4) Take it with a grain of salt
   5) One's cup of tea
   6) Clean one's plate

2. Pair work

   Discuss your thoughts about the definitions with a partner.

3. Match the expressions with the meanings.

1) Food for thought	a. One's favorite thing
2) Clean one's plate	b. Not be serious
3) One's cup of tea	c. Finish one's food
4) Eat it up	d. Something to think about
5) Take it with a grain of salt	e. Enjoy it
6) Couch potato	f. Lazy person

4. Group work

   Do you have similar idioms or expressions in your own language? Brainstorm in groups of three to four, about expressions of speech you use in your native language. Share your list with the class.

What in the World?

Food and eating form very important parts of every culture around the world. Each culture has habits and customs for eating and preparing foods.

1. Match each famous dish to its country.

1) Sweet and Sour Soup	a. Morocco
2) Sangria	b. Mexico
3) Sashimi	c. Korea
4) Lasagna	d. America
5) Quesadilla	e. Spain
6) Dal Soup	f. France
7) Baguette	g. Italy
8) Apple Pie	h. India
9) Kimchi	i. China
10) Mint tea	j. Japan

NOTES:

2. Pair work

Take turns reading these passages with a partner. Use the following sentence for help:

example ____________ (food) is/are from ___________ (country). Hamburgers are from the United States.

NOTES:

Unit 5

Fit as a Fiddle

Unit 05 Fit as a Fiddle

Conversation

- Talk about health and wellness
- Talk about ailments and medication
- Talk about the body

Situations

- Visit a doctor or clinic
- Go to the hospital
- Talk about the body

Vocabulary Preview

Ill / sick	Well	Healthy
Fit / fitness	Sore throat	Runny nose
Sneeze (verb and noun)	Cough (verb and noun)	Allergy
Influenza / flu	Common cold / cold	Injured
(Body part) Ache	Digestive system	Circulatory system
Nervous system	Respiratory system	Reproductive system
Endocrine	Specialist (doctor)	

Let's Get Started

1. Review this list of vocabulary words. Translate the English words into Korean.

▶ English	▶▶ Korean	▶ English	▶▶ Korean
ill / sick		common cold / cold	
well		injured	
healthy		digestive system	
fit / fitness		circulatory system	
sore throat		nervous system	
runny nose		respiratory system	
sneeze		endocrine system	
cough		reproductive system	
allergy		specialist (doctor)	
influenza / flu		(body part) ache	

NOTES:

2. Match the questions with the answers.

1) Does your throat hurt?	a. Yes, I saw a specialist yesterday.
2) Have you been to the doctor?	b. No. I am sick.
3) Do you have a cold?	c. They are in the respiratory system.
4) Are you well?	d. They are in the endocrine system.
5) What was he doing?	e. No, it's not a cold. I think I have allergies.
6) What body system are the lungs in?	f. It is in the digestive system.
7) What body system are hormones in?	g. He was sneezing and coughing.
8) What body system is the stomach in?	h. Yes, it's very sore.

3. Pair Work

Ask and answer the questions from part 2 with your partner.

NOTES:

4. Classify the body systems with related words in the box below. Write the names of the words beneath the correct category.

Body Systems

Endocrine		Respiratory
Nervous	Digestive	Circulatory

heart	testosterone	lungs	arteries
brain	airway	small intestine	nerves
stomach	veins	colon	hypothalamus
estrogen	spinal cord	hormones	pancreas

5. Pair work

Add three more related words to any category. Have your partner help you.

6. Group work

To find out if you were right, ask two classmates their answers. Compare classifications.

Say It Right

Listen to the following passages about health and wellness. Notice the stress and intonation of each sentence. Audio

❶ Common symptoms of a cold are: a runny nose, sore throat and a cough. Many people feel tired, too. You should see a doctor if you think you are sick. They can prescribe medication for you. If you rest, eat well and take your medicine, you can be feeling better in no time at all.

❷ Exercise is an important part of maintaining a healthy body. When we lead active lives, we build strong and fit bodies. Active people get sick less frequently and have more energy. Regular exercise leads to a strong heart, healthy lungs and a sharp mind.

❸ Eating healthfully helps the body fight disease. Fresh fruit and vegetables are an important part of our daily food intake. They contain valuable vitamins and minerals that make the body strong. They give us extra energy to make it through a busy day. A vitamin deficiency can often lead to serious health problems.

❹ Blood is often misunderstood and under-appreciated. Blood is vital and helps deliver oxygen to our organs. Blood is a massive transportation system in the body. It helps move cells of all kinds to all systems of the body.

1. Listen again. This time, underline words that are stressed and emphasized by the speaker's voice.

2. Pair work

   Practice each statement from part 1 with your partner.

Speaking

Listen to the conversation between Peggy and Brian. Answer the following questions. Audio

Peggy : Hey, Brian. You look great. How do you stay so fit and healthy?

Brian : Well, thanks. I try to stay active, exercise regularly and eat well. It's not easy, but being healthy is important to me.

Peggy : It's important to me, too, but I can't seem to manage everything. I am tired all of the time.

Brian : Well, if you are just starting to change your lifestyle, try one change at a time. Start with resting 6~7 hours a night. That is the best way to maintain a healthy body.

Peggy : Well, I think I am resting enough. Plus, I drink a lot of water everyday. I still feel tired though.

Brian : So, you don't feel well. Do you have any other symptoms?

Peggy : Symptoms? Like problems? Sure. I have sore muscles in my neck and back. My eyes itch, and my nose is runny.

Brian : Ha ha. I see. Do you feel better or worse when you go outside?

Peggy : I feel worse. I don't spend a lot of time outdoors, so I'm not walking enough. Then, I feel worse because I am not active.

Brian : I think I know what's wrong with you.

Peggy : Really? Am I sick? Could I die? Do you think it's serious?

Brian : Relax. I think you have seasonal allergies. You are allergic to something outside, like grasses or pollen.

Peggy : That's all? What a relief. It could have been the flu, a cold or even death knocking on my door. . .

Brian : Oh, calm down. Go to a pharmacy and get an antihistamine. I have a feeling this isn't terminal.

1. What does Peggy want to know?

2. Pair work

Practice the conversation with a partner.

3. Answer True or False for the statements about the conversation.

1)	Peggy has cancer.	T	F
2)	Brian is fit and healthy.	T	F
3)	Peggy's eyes itch and her nose is runny.	T	F
4)	Brian told Peggy to rest 7-8 hours a night.	T	F
5)	Peggy should go to a doctor for medicine.	T	F
6)	Brain thinks Peggy has seasonal allergies.	T	F
7)	Peggy will go to a pharmacy for an antihistamine.	T	F
8)	Peggy spends too much time outdoors.	T	F
9)	Brian is always feeling tired.	T	F
10)	Staying healthy is important to Brian and Peggy.	T	F

4. Answer the following questions about the conversation.

1) What symptoms does Peggy have?

2) What might Peggy be allergic to?

3) Does Peggy feel better when she is inside or outside?

5. Pair work

Ask and answer the questions from part 4 with your partner.

Listening Comprehension

Listen to this short story. Listen for the main idea and details. Audio

Flip-flops, the sandal-like footwear most of us wear to the beach, may be bad for our health, according to a study carried out by the American College of Sports Medicine. The report showed that walking in flip-flops can trigger aches and pains all over the body, not just making our feet sore. It goes so far as to say that flip-flops are the most damaging type of shoes for our health, even worse than high heels. Report author Justin Shroyer stated: "We found that when people walk in flip-flops, they alter their gait, which can result in problems and pain from the foot up into the hips and lower back." He explained that people changed their walking style because they were "very concerned about stubbing their toes" and wanted to make sure the flip-flop stayed put on the foot and did not go flying off.

The research involved 39 male and female graduates. They were videoed while walking in flip-flops and in athletic shoes. The researchers compared the length of people's stride and limb angles when people wore the different footwear. They discovered that people in flip-flops took shorter steps, gripped more with their toes and moved their ankles in a wider angle. All of these changes to our walking style cause unnatural shocks to our joints. This can create stresses, which can lead to serious injury, if they are repeated over a long period of time. Estimates are that the average person takes 15,000 steps each day. Even small, unnatural changes to a healthy walking style can be multiplied thousands of times if we wear flip-flops all day. The researchers advised wearing flip-flops for short periods of time only.

1. Which title best fits the story? Circle your answer.

   1) Flip-Flops Are Better Than High Heels

   2) Flip-Flops Are Beach Footwear

   3) Flip-Flops May Cause Damage to Our Health

2. Read the story out loud to your partner. Practice slowly and focus on your accent and pronunciation.

3. Pair work

   Which style of footwear is your favorite? Ask your partner.

4. Mark true or false for the following statements about the story.

1) Flip flops are comfortable and easy to walk in.	T	F
2) People grip more with their toes in flip-flops.	T	F
3) Flip-flops should never be worn.	T	F
4) 39 athletes were videoed for the flip-flop research.	T	F
5) Each person takes an average of 15,000 steps a day.	T	F
6) The study says high-heels are the worst footwear.	T	F

NOTES:

5. Answer the following questions about the story.

1) Are flip-flops easy to walk in? Why or why not?

2) How are flip-flops dangerous for our health?

3) Would you consider NOT wearing flip-flops after reading this article?

4) Do you ever wear uncomfortable shoes? Why or why not?

5) What did researchers compare while studying flip-flops?

6) What does 'gait' mean? Look in paragraph 1, line 7 for context clues.

6. In your opinion . . .

What is the most attractive style of shoes for a man or a woman? Label the shoe styles from 1 (most attractive) to 5 (least attractive).

	Man		Woman
a.	_____	sandals	_____
b.	_____	high heels	_____
c.	_____	flip-flops	_____
d.	_____	boots	_____
e.	_____	athletic shoes	_____
f.	_____	slippers	_____

7. Group work

Look around the class. What style of shoes are your classmates wearing? What is popular? Why do you think so?

Food for Thought

1. Review these idiomatic expressions. What do you think they mean?

   1) Break-neck speed
   2) Stick your neck out
   3) Be up to your neck
   4) A pain in the neck
   5) Breath down someone's neck
   6) Save someone's neck

2. Pair work

   Discuss your thoughts about the definitions with a partner.

3. Match the expressions with the meanings.

1) Save someone's neck	a. Help someone from a bad situation
2) Break-neck speed	b. Invade someone's personal space
3) Breath down someone's neck	c. Annoying situation / person
4) Stick your neck out	d. Have a lot of something ; work, etc.
5) A pain in the neck	e. Exceptionally fast
6) Be up to your neck	f. Risk yourself for someone or something

4. Group work

   Do you have similar idioms or expressions in your own language? Brainstorm in groups of three to four, about expressions of speech you use in your native language. Share your list with the class.

What in the World?

1. Are you sick or are you injured? In English, the words sick and injured are often misused. Use this guide to help you navigate when and how to use each expression.

Sick

Sick is used for illness or health problems that are generally *inside* of the body. They mostly have a viral, bacterial or natural cause. Most have a cure, while some are terminal.

Expressions :	Examples :
I am sick.	cancer
I feel sick.	cold
Are you sick?	flu
Do you feel sick?	upset stomach
	sore throat
	food poisoning

Injured

Injured is used for a condition that happens to the body. This is usually on the outside of the body. Injuries can also occur to the inside of the body due to force or impact coming from the outside. Injuries generally heal with time. Some cause permanent damage.

Expressions :	Examples:
I am injured.	cuts
I have an injury.	bruises
Are you injured?	broken bones
Do you have an injury?	joint sprains
	back / neck aches
	general body pains

2. Pair work

Take turns asking your partner if they are sick or injured. Answer yes, and then explain what is wrong with you. Ask and answer three questions.

Example A : Are you sick or injured?
B : I am sick.
A : What is wrong with you? / What is the matter with you?
B : I have a cold.

NOTES:

Unit 6

Home, Sweet Home

Unit 06 Home, Sweet Home

Conversation

- Discuss homes around the world
- Talk about campus and student housing
- Talk about apartment and house hunting

Situations

- Find a new house
- Rent an apartment
- Ask about other peoples' homes

Vocabulary Preview

Garage	Veranda	Patio	Basement
Attic	Living room	Family room	Great room
Mudroom	Hallway	Real estate office	Real estate agent
Property	Stilts	Hut	Yurt
Traditional	Modern	Commercial	Residential

Let's Get Started

1. Review this list of vocabulary words. Translate the English words into Korean.

▶ English	▶▶ Korean	▶ English	▶▶ Korean
garage		real estate office	
veranda		real estate agent	
patio		property	
basement		stilts	
attic		hut	
living room		yurt	
family room		traditional	
great room		modern	
mudroom		commercial	
hallway		residential	

NOTES:

2. Answer the following questions with the vocabulary words from part 1.

1) What is the name of property where businesses can operate?

2) What is the name of the room where you leave shoes and possibly do laundry?

3) What is the name of the small space above the main floor of a house?

4) What type of house is a simple structure, usually made of organic materials?

5) Where do you go when you want to buy a new house? Who can help you?

3. Pair Work. Use the questions and answers in part 2 to interview your partner.

4. Match the two columns to make common home-related phrases.

1) Visit ...	a. the garage
2) Buy ...	b. in the mudroom
3) Clean ...	c. in the family room
4) Watch television ...	d. a real estate office
5) Take off your shoes ...	e. a modern house
6) Prefer ...	f. some commercial property

5. Pair work

Use the questions, phrases and nouns from the box to ask and answer questions using the vocabulary words from part 1.

Example How many *bathrooms* are there? There are three *bathrooms.*

Questions	Nouns
How many ____ are there?	bathrooms
Is there a ____?	bedrooms
Does the house have a ___?	space (meters / feet / pyeong)
How much ____ is there?	garage /
Does it have a ____?	patio / veranda / attic
Can I see a house with ___?	

NOTES:

Say It Right

1. Listen to the following statements related to houses. Notice the intonation and emphasis of each sentence. Audio

   1) I would like to see a bigger house, please.
   2) My dream house would be on stilts, over the water.
   3) If I'm not careful, I may end up living in a hut.
   4) I left my cell phone in the basement.

2. Listen again. This time, underline the words in each sentence that are emphasized. Audio

3. Write three statements using the expressions of like / dislike and verbs with the place names from the box below.

   Example I would love to travel to Ghana.

   1)
   2)
   3)

Expressions of desire	Adjective	Type of Home
I would love	huge	house
I never want	modest	apartment
I would hate	modern	hut
I heard that	traditional	yurt
I feel that	eco-friendly	villa
I like	simple	mansion
I dislike	beautiful	shack

Speaking

Listen to the conversation between Corey and Hyung Chul. Answer the following questions. Audio

Corey : I was thinking about my dream house today. Where do you want to live?

Hyung Chul : Well, to be honest, I never really thought about it until now. Give me a minute.

Corey : Sure. I think out of all home styles, I just want something simple. I don't need a mansion or a tropical bungalow on stilts over the water.

Hyung Chul : Really, I think something near the water sounds great.

Corey : Is that your dream home?

Hyung Chul : No. Really, I can't tell you. You'll laugh at me.

Corey : You know me better than that. I won't laugh, I promise.

Hyung Chul : Okay, I have always wanted to move to the desert and live in one of those round tent-like houses. What are they called again?

Corey : A yurt? You want to live in a yurt?

Hyung Chul : Yup. That's the one. I want to live in a yurt. They are very eco-friendly, you know.

Corey : You can have whatever makes you happy, but I want a house. Not too big, not too small, just a comfortable house to call home.

Hyung Chul : Fair enough Corey. I'll take the yurt and you take the house.

Corey : So, will you visit me when you come from the dessert?

Hyung Chul : Sure, as long as I can bring my yurt to the city!

1. Where do they dream of living?

2. Pair work

Practice the conversation with a partner.

3. Answer True or False for the statements about the conversation.

1) Corey wants a comfortable house.	T	F
2) Hyung Chul wants to live in the mountains.	T	F
3) Yurts are eco-friendly.	T	F
4) Corey was thinking about homes today.	T	F
5) Corey wants to live near the water.	T	F
6) Hyung Chul thinks yurts are great.	T	F
7) Hyung Chul will visit Corey in the desert.	T	F
8) Hyung Chul will bring his yurt to the city.	T	F
9) They have different styles of dream homes.	T	F
10) Corey wants a very small house.	T	F

NOTES:

4. Answer the following questions about the conversation.

1) Where does Corey want to live?

2) What is a yurt?

3) What kind of house does Hyung Chul want?

4) What style of house does Corey not need?

5) What does Hyung Chul have to do in order to visit Corey?

5. Pair work

Where would you like to live? Which style of home is your dream home? Is it near the water, in the mountains or in the desert? Discuss it with a partner.

NOTES:

Listening Comprehension

Listen to this short story. Listen for the main idea and details. Audio

Cuba is changing quickly. Cubans can now build their own houses for the first time in 50 years. The country's president, Raul Castro, has announced changes to help the nation's housing shortage. For the past five decades, people had to rely on the government to provide them with houses. There was no such thing as housing loans or a property market. The new reforms will allow people to get loans to build their own homes. There will still be many restrictions. All new properties must follow strict building guidelines. The government has announced dimensions for new houses that all architects must stick to. Mr. Castro explained his decision live on television, telling his people: "I've given you this amount of space.... Now build your little home with whatever you can."

Housing has become a serious problem in Cuba. There are now too few houses for people to live in. Overcrowding is reaching record levels as more and more people live with their families in tiny properties. Cuba's government has had difficulty keeping to its targets of building 100,000 new homes per year. The situation has been made worse by three huge hurricanes that hit the island in 2008. Hundreds of thousands of homes were destroyed in the fierce winds and driving rain. One potential Cuban homeowner, Jose Santana, was delighted with the news. "My dream to have my own home may soon come true," he said. This may be easier said than done. The average wage in Cuba is just $17 a month, and most building materials are only available on the black market.

1. Which title best fits the story? Circle your answer.

   1) Cubans are Poor

   2) Good News for Cubans

   3) Castro is a Great Man

2. Read the story out loud to your partner. Practice slowly and focus on your accent and pronunciation.

3. Answer the questions about the story.

   1) How long has it been since Cubans could build their own homes?

   2) Who is the president of Cuba?

   3) How many new homes does the country want to build?

   4) What is the average monthly wage of a person in Cuba?

   5) What are some of the restrictions Cubans must follow?

4. In your opinion

   Answer the following questions using your feelings, thoughts and ideas.

   1) Is it better for the government to provide housing for its citizens or for the people to build their own houses?

   2) What changes can Raul Castro make to improve housing conditions in Cuba?

   3) How would you feel if you lost your home, in a hurricane or storm, like many Cubans have?

Food for Thought

1. Review these idiomatic expressions. What do you think they mean?

   1) Make yourself at home
   2) The homestretch
   3) It's on the house
   4) A home away from home
   5) Drive it home
   6) Until the cows come home

2. Pair work

   Discuss your thoughts about the definitions with a partner.

3. Match the expressions with the meanings.

1) It's on the house	a. very late at night
2) A home away from home	b. be comfortable
3) The homestretch	c. spend a lot of time somewhere
4) Drive it home	d. reinforce it
5) Make yourself at home	e. the end or terminal point
6) Until the cows come home	f. free

4. Group work

   Do you have similar idioms or expressions in your own language? Brainstorm in groups of three to four, about expressions of speech you use in your native language. Share your list with the class.

What in the World?

Audio

People all over the world live in different kinds of houses. Some are modern, while others are traditional. Listen about these four interesting homes. Then ask your partner which of these four homes they would prefer to live in. Find out why they prefer that style.

❶ The Plains Indians of North America lived in tepees. The frame was made from long wooden poles fastened together at the top. The opposite ends were spread out to form a circle. Then they were covered with a tent of animal skin and tied to the ground. The outsides of the teepees were decorated. This style was convenient because the teepees were easy to move for hunting.

❷ On the Tonle Sap River in Cambodia, homes are built on stilts above the river. This helps protect the homes when the river floods.

❸ People in the southern part of the Philippines use to live in tree houses. This viewpoint allowed them to see enemies, animals and poisonous snakes. The air was also cooler and drier high up in the trees. Tree houses are now used for resting and holding meetings.

④ In the southern part of Morocco, houses are made of bricks. Water is mixed with clay soil and left to dry in the hot desert sun. Clay is used to paste the bricks together, one by one, until an entire house is built. The brick construction helps to regulate the inside temperature of the house, even if it's very hot outside. The downfall to brick homes is that they do not withstand earthquakes very well.

Unit 7

You Owe Me

Go Native!
Conversation
for English Language Learners

Unit 07

You Owe Me

Conversation

- Speak and read large numbers
- Talk about items while shopping
- Talk about budgets
- Discuss expenses

Situations

- Go shopping
- Create a budget
- Manage monthly expenses

Vocabulary Preview

Rent, Utilities, Debit card, Credit card, Personal check, Cash, Store credit, Gift card / certificate, Antique shop, Barbershop, Beauty salon, Convenience store, Department store, Newspaper stand, Oriental medicine store, Shoe store, Stationary store, Souvenir store, Craft store, Bookstore

Let's Get Started

1. Review this list of vocabulary words. Translate the English words into Korean.

▸ English	▸▸ Korean	▸ English	▸▸ Korean
rent		beauty salon	
utilities		convenience store	
debit card		department store	
credit card		newspaper stand	
personal check		oriental medicine store	
cash		shoe store	
store credit		stationary store	
gift card / certificate		souvenir store	
antique shop		craft store	
barber shop		bookstore	

2. Answer the following questions with the vocabulary words from part 1.

1) Where can you buy a snack and a drink?

2) Where can you buy Chinese medicine?

3) Where can you buy Western medicine?

4) What is another word for paper money?

5) Which card automatically deducts funds from your bank account?

3. Pair Work. Use the questions and answers in part 2 to interview your partner.

4. Seek the words. Find the vocabulary words from the box below in the puzzle.

You Owe Me!														
W	V	C	W	C	I	U	D	S	R	M	Z	C	W	J
O	B	O	Y	A	E	N	X	E	U	S	E	H	F	I
R	A	N	Q	R	T	R	P	I	B	V	B	E	Z	P
I	P	V	R	D	A	A	T	T	R	I	D	C	Z	B
E	T	E	D	I	P	N	S	I	U	E	T	K	A	D
N	F	N	R	S	N	T	O	L	F	U	N	R	E	N
T	I	I	W	S	U	E	N	I	Z	I	B	T	U	A
A	G	E	V	R	O	F	V	T	T	E	C	P	Q	T
L	N	N	E	G	K	N	D	U	R	A	O	A	I	S
S	L	C	R	N	O	L	A	S	O	H	T	D	T	A
J	B	E	A	U	T	Y	H	L	S	S	E	S	N	E
B	O	O	K	S	T	O	R	E	V	R	H	S	A	C
C	R	A	F	T	P	E	N	I	C	I	D	E	M	A
T	N	E	M	T	R	A	P	E	D	S	H	O	E	S
J	C	T	N	J	W	B	R	Q	B	U	Z	N	C	A

Vocabulary

ANTIQUE	UTILITIES	BEAUTY	BOOKSTORE	CARD
CASH	CERTIFICATE	CHECK	CONVENIENCE	CRAFT
CREDIT	DEPARTMENT	GIFT	MEDICINE	SALON
NEWSPAPER	ORIENTAL	PERSONAL	RENT	SHOE
SHOP	SOUVENIR	STAND	STATIONARY	STORE

Say It Right

1. Listen to the following large numbers being read aloud. Pay attention to the place-values. Audio

   1) 1,953
   2) 546,927
   3) 2,874,089
   4) 475,872,908
   5) $47,000.25

2. Listen to the following large numbers. Write them down as you listen. Audio

   1)
   2)
   3)
   4)
   5)

3. Write the numbers the way in which you speak them.

   Example 3,935: three thousand nine hundred thirty-five

   1) 1,900
   2) 651,915
   3) 1,653,092
   4) $547,249.44

MONEY TALKS

1. Where there is a comma, a place-value is spoken.

   1,200 = one thousand two hundred

2. Think in 3's ; each place-value has three numbers.

   456,900 = four hundred fifty-six thousand nine hundred

3. If there is a comma, it is a large number. If there is NO comma, it is a year.

   1,999 = one thousand nine hundred ninety-nine

   1999 = nineteen ninety nine

4. While the dollar or won sign comes first, you speak it only before the decimal point.

   $16.25 = sixteen dollars and twenty-five cents

NOTES:

Speaking

Listen to the conversation between Soon Wong and Mae. Answer the following questions. Audio

Soon Wong: Did you pay the utilities yet this month?

Mae : Yes. I paid them. The total amount was $154.87.

Soon Wong: Okay. I'll take care of the rent later today. It's difficult to stick to a budget and manage our monthly expenses.

Mae : Well, frankly speaking, after the rent, utilities and grocery bills, there isn't a lot left over for entertainment.

Soon Wong: That's true, but we still get to shop at our favorite department stores for shoes and clothes. You also spend a lot of cash at the beauty salon.

Mae : I guess I do spend a fair amount. If I cut back at the salon, you can buy that watch from the antique shop that you like so much.

Soon Wong: Really? You would do that for me?

Mae : Yes, darling, I would.

Soon Wong: So what other things can we do to manage our expenses?

Mae : We received a lot of gift cards at our wedding; maybe we should use them instead of the credit cards.

Soon Wong: Yea, didn't we get one for the bookstore? We can re-gift that to your sister for her birthday.

Mae : Great idea! She loves books and stationary.

Soon Wong: Do you think we can pay the rent with a gift card from the shoe store?

Mae : You have a great sense of humor; that's why I married you!

1. What are Mae and Soon Wong trying to do?

2. Pair work

Practice the conversation with a partner.

3. Answer True or False for the statements about the conversation.

1) Soon Wong and Mae are married.	T	F
2) Mae paid the rent already.	T	F
3) Soon Wong wants a new watch.	T	F
4) Mae's sister loves books.	T	F
5) Mae spends a lot of money at the salon.	T	F
6) Mae and Soon Wong shop at the outlet store.	T	F
7) Mae and Soon Wong have a budget.	T	F
8) Soon Wong will pay the rent today.	T	F
9) The utilities cost $145.87.	T	F
10) Mae uses her debit card at the salon.	T	F

4. Answer the following questions about the conversation.

1) Where do Soon Wong and Mae buy clothes and shoes?

2) What should Mae do so that Soon Wong can buy his watch?

3) Why do Soon Wong and Mae have a lot of gift cards?

4) How will Soon Wong and Mae manage their monthly expenses?

Listening Comprehension

Listen to this short story. Listen for the main idea and details.

Plastic cards are the UK's favorite way to pay for goods and services, according to a new report by APACS, the body that monitors payments in Britain. Spending on plastic cards overtook cash in 2004 and has continued growing ever since. British consumers' love of plastic means that spending on credit and debit cards has risen over the past decade. A little under a third of total consumer spending is now charged to cards. Plastic transactions increased to a record $600bn last year. APACS director of communications Sandra Quinn said: "The last 10 years have seen a rapid rise in the popularity of plastic, with debit cards showing particularly strong growth." She added: "Consumers enjoy the ease and convenience plastic cards bring, and today most retailers and supermarkets take plastic, as do an increasing number of professional service providers."

Last year we saw new 'smart card' technology introduced into the world of card payments. However, these technological advances have not stopped an increasing reliance on plastic, which is responsible for the rising mountains of debt British people now have. In the first three months of this year almost 17,000 people were declared bankrupt – a 10 percent rise on the previous year. There is also a parallel, worrying trend regarding the opportunities plastic creates for fraud. In 2006, conmen stole almost a billion dollars using stolen cards and personal information. Soon, people will be carrying a single card in their wallet, which will combine debit and credit cards and other financial transactions. This is another step toward a cashless society, but one that might increase personal debt and credit card fraud.

1. Which title best fits the story? Circle your answer.

   1) A Cash-only Society in the UK

   2) Plastic Replacing Cash in the UK

   3) Cash Replacing Plastic in the UK

2. Read the story out loud to your partner. Practice slowly and focus on your accent and pronunciation.

3. Answer the questions about the story.

   1) What does 'plastic' refer to?

   2) What percentage of spending in Britain involves credit cards?

   3) How many people in Britain filed for bankruptcy?

   4) What is smart card technology?

   5) Will credit cards increase or decrease the level of fraud in Britain?

4. In your opinion

   Answer the following questions using your feelings, thoughts and ideas.

   1) Do you think credit cards are more convenient than cash? Why or why not?

   2) What are some of the dangers of using a lot of plastic?

   3) Why do you think that credit cards are becoming more popular?

5. Pair work

   Ask these questions to your partner. Share your own answers with your partner.

Food for Thought

1. Review these idiomatic expressions. What do you think they mean?

   1) Bet your bottom dollar

   2) How the cookie crumbles

   3) Stretch your dollar

   4) At the drop of a dime

   5) Bring home the bacon

   6) Pay the piper

2. Pair work

   Discuss your thoughts about the definitions with a partner.

3. Match the expressions with the meanings.

1) Pay the piper	a. Be absolutely sure
2) Bring home the bacon	b. Be frugal with money
3) At the drop of a dime	c. The end result
4) Stretch your dollar	d. Immediately or without hesitation
5) How the cookie crumbles	e. Financially support your family
6) Bet your bottom dollar	f. Accept the consequence

4. Group work

   Do you have similar idioms or expressions in your own language? Brainstorm in groups of three to four, about expressions of speech you use in your native language. Share your list with the class.

What in the World?

Money makes the world go around. Listen to the following passages about the history of money. Audio

❶ Many items have been used for money, such as scarce metal, shells, barley, beads, and other things thought to have value in a culture. The use of money, in some form, can be traced back over 100,000 years.

❷ In places where metal was readily available, standardized coins became the preferred money of choice. Coins were used instead of cattle, salt or other commodities. They were easy to carry and easy to trade for other goods and services.

❸ Representative money is when a bank issued a receipt for a deposit. It was a guarantee that the deposit of wealth would be returned to the bearer. The receipt became paper bills that were issued by the governments and central banks. This system was used in the United States until 1971.

❹ In 1971, the United States switched to fiat currency. Fiat currency is a paper bill that is not guaranteed by a reserve or any commodity. The "money" itself is given value by the government. This form of money is what most countries use today.

❺ Credit money is used with fiat money. There is no difference for the user. Banks lend to people and companies. The banks don't lend "actual" wealth. They lend a "credit" of wealth, which has no real value. This increases the money supply, but not the actual amount of wealth available to people. People repay this credit with fiat money.

1. Pair work

Take turns reading these passages with a partner.

2. Group work

Ask two classmates which kind of money they use, how often they use it and why.

NOTES:

Unit 8

Time Flies When You're Having Fun

Unit 08 Time Flies When You're Having Fun

Conversation

- Talk about past experiences
- Use past, future and present expressions

Situations

- Discuss the past
- Talk about personal facts

Vocabulary Preview

Early	Late	Afternoon	Day
Evening	Lunchtime	Midday	Midnight
Midmorning	Night	Sunrise	Dusk
Sunset	Wee hours	Since	Ago
Until	Some	Most	

Let's Get Started

1. Review this list of vocabulary words. Translate the English words into Korean.

▶ English	▶▶ Korean	▶ English	▶▶ Korean
early		sunrise	
late		dusk	
afternoon		sunset	
day		wee hours	
evening		everyone	
lunchtime		since	
midday		ago	
midnight		until	
midmorning		some	
night		most	

2. Write a sentence with the vocabulary words from part 1.

1) Everyone :

2) Since :

3) Dusk :

4) Lunchtime :

5) Midday :

3. Pair Work

Read your sentences from part 2 to your partner. Listen to their sentences

4. How much do you know about your classmates? Look at the following statements and check (✔) the ones you think are true.

1) Some people did homework last night. ____
2) Some people watched a movie last night. ____
3) Most people were still sleeping at 4:00 in the morning. ____
4) Everyone was eating breakfast at 8:30 in the morning. ____
5) At least two people have had a part-time job. ____
6) Everyone was dating someone last month. ____
7) Most people watched TV until 10:00 last night. ____
8) Most people have lived in their house for at least 5 years. ____

5. To find out if you were right, ask two classmates their answers. Write their answers below. Use expressions from the box below for help.

1) ____
2) ____
3) ____
4) ____
5) ____
6) ____
7) ____
8) ____

Expressions of Time

Questions	Statements
What were you doing...?	I (watched TV) until (8:00 last night).
How long have you...?	I have been (living at my house) for (14 years).
What time did you...?	I (went to bed) at (midnight) (last night).
Have you ever...?	I have had (a part-time job) since (I was 20).
Did you _______ last night?	I (watched TV) (yesterday).
yesterday?	
last month?	
this morning?	

NOTES:

Say It Right

1. Listen to the following statement. Notice the stress and intonation of each statement and how it changes. The underlined word carries the vocal stress and emphasis. How are they different? Audio

   1) *I* hate dirty dogs. (Someone else likes them, just not the subject.)

   2) I *hate* dirty dogs. (Really, the subject has a strong dislike for them.)

   3) I hate *dirty* dogs. (However, the subject does like clean dogs.)

   4) I hate dirty *dogs*. (Other dirty things are okay, just not dogs.)

2. Listen to the conversation between Hana and Penny. Audio

   Circle the expression you hear.

   Hana : What were you doing before this class?

   Penny : I was sleeping before I came here.

   Hana : Time has really flown by. Most people have really changed.

   Penny : You can say that again.

3. Pair work

   Practice each statement from part 3 with your partner.

Speaking

Listen to the conversation between Daniel and Marianne. Answer the following questions. Audio

Daniel : Did you study for the English exam last night?

Marianne : Of course I did. I was up until the wee hours of the morning.

Daniel : Really? I studied for about five hours. Then, I called it quits.

Marianne : Only five hours? That doesn't seem like much.

Daniel : This time last week I was studying, too. I have been studying for this exam since last month.

Marianne : Good thinking, Daniel. You are always ahead of the game.

Daniel : No, I just don't like staying up until dawn. It's better to take an exam after a good rest.

Marianne : That is what I heard but I can never seem to be prepared.

Daniel : You have to plan ahead. I start studying about four weeks before a major exam. Little by little, I learn the material and I get to sleep the night before the exam.

Marianne : How long have you been preparing this way?

Daniel : I started studying this way about two years ago.

Marianne : Have you noticed any improvements since you changed your study habits?

Daniel : Sure. My scores have improved a lot and I never feel the stress my friends feel right before the exam.

Marianne : Well, it's too late for me this time around, but next time, I'm trying it your way!

1. What is Marianne's problem?

2. Pair work

Practice the conversation with a partner.

3. Answer True of False for the statements about the conversation.

1) Daniel's scores have improved.	T	F
2) Marianne studied until dawn.	T	F
3) Marianne studied until the middle of the night.	T	F
4) Daniel likes to plan ahead.	T	F
5) Marianne thinks Daniel's study habits are bad.	T	F
6) Daniel started to study three weeks ago.	T	F
7) Marianne had never studied for an exam before.	T	F
8) Daniel likes to stay up late.	T	F
9) Daniel studied for five hours.	T	F
10) Marianne will try Daniel's technique next time.	T	F

4. Four phrases are underlined in the conversation. What do they mean? Write the answers below. Use context clues from the conversation for help.

1) <u>Called it quits</u> :

2) <u>Doesn't seem like much</u> :

3) <u>Ahead of the game</u> :

4) <u>This time around</u> :

Listening Comprehension

Listen to this short story. Listen for the main idea and details. Audio

A leading US scientist has predicted that computers will be as intelligent as humans by 2029. Futurologist Dr. Ray Kurzweil told the American Association for the Advancement of Science that in the near future, machine intelligence will overtake the power of the human brain. He said that within two decades computers will be able to think quicker than humans. Dr. Kurzweil painted a picture of us having tiny robots called nanobots implanted in our brain to boost our intelligence and health. He told reporters that these microscopic nanobots would work with our brains to make us think faster and give us more powerful memories. Kurzweil explained that we are already "a human machine civilization" and that the upcoming technology "will be a further extension of that."

Dr. Kurzweil was one of 18 top intellectuals asked by the US National Academy of Engineering to identify our greatest technological challenges. Other experts included Google founder Larry Page and the human genome pioneer Dr. Craig Venter. Kurzweil has a very impressive background in science and innovation. He was an innovator in various fields of computing, including the technology behind CDs. He also pioneered automatic speech recognition by machines. He predicts the pace of new inventions will increase greatly from now, saying: "...the next half century will see 32 times more technical progress than the past half century." This means scenes from science fiction movies, like *Blade Runner*, *The Terminator* and *I Robot*, will become more and more a part of our everyday lives.

1. Which title best fits the story? Circle your answer.

    1) Computers to Out-Think Man by 2029

    2) Micro-Bots Will Live in Our Brains

    3) Computers are the Root of All Evil

2. Read the story out loud to your partner. Practice slowly and focus on your accent and pronunciation.

3. Pair work

    How has technology changed your life in the last 5 years?

4. Answer the questions about the story.

    1) How can nanobots benefit humans?

    2) What are some of Dr. Kurzweil's accomplishments?

    3) What does he predict will happen in the next half century?

    4) What is the main topic of this article?

NOTES:

5. Match the phrases from the story.

1) computers will be as intelligent	a. part of our everyday lives
2) overtake the power	b. 18 top intellectuals
3) tiny robots	c. powerful memories
4) make us think faster and give us more	d. as humans
5) technology will be a further	e. called nanobots
6) one of	f. challenges
7) identify our greatest technological	g. speech recognition
8) a very impressive	h. extension of that
9) He also pioneered automatic	i. of the human brain
10) more and more a	j. background in science

6. Pair work

Rank these possible reasons for putting a nanobot into your body. Change partners and share your ideas and findings. 1 is most important, 6 is least important.

a. _____ to live to be 125

b. _____ to play an instrument like a concert performer

c. _____ to speak a new language fluently

d. _____ to play computer games like the world's best player

e. _____ to be happy all day, every day

f. _____ to look very young for all of your life

Food for Thought

1. Review these idiomatic expressions. What do you think they mean?

   1) Time is of the essence
   2) No time like the present
   3) Time is money
   4) Time flies
   5) Grin and bear it
   6) Life and limb

2. Pair work

   Discuss your thoughts about the definitions with a partner.

3. Match the expressions with the meanings.

1) Time is money	a. Time passes very quickly
2) Time flies	b. Tolerate something unpleasant
3) No time like the present	c. Risking a lot / risk one's life
4) Grin and bear it	d. The situation is time sensitive
5) Time is of the essence	e. Now is the best time
6) Life and limb	f. Time is very valuable

4. Group work

   Do you have similar idioms or expressions in your own language? Brainstorm in groups of three to four, about expressions of speech you use in your native language. Share your list with the class.

What in the World?

In every country and on every continent, people have different concepts of time. If you are invited to an informal gathering at a friend's house at 9:00 at night, what time should you arrive? It all depends on where you are!

The United States

Be on time or be a little early, but don't come too late, especially if dinner is being served. It's considered terribly rude to arrive late for dinner. In fact, you might even prevent the party from getting started. If the invitation says 9:00, be there at 9:00. If you will be late, call to let your host know.

Korea

While you shouldn't arrive too early, Koreans are flexible a few minutes either way. If the invitation says 9:00, then 8:45 or 9:30 is generally considered acceptable. It's not so rude to arrive late. If you are lucky, the party is just getting started.

Costa Rica

It's Tico Time! Tico Time refers to the fact that Costa Rica runs on a different clock. If the invitation says 9:00, don't consider arriving until 10:00, at the earliest. If you arrive at 9 o'clock, your host will be offended as they will not be ready for you yet. Arrive late, in fact, the later the better!

Business is business···

As globalization brings us closer together in a number of ways, we shouldn't forget about international business conduct. While it's best to arrive at least 5~10 minutes early for business meetings, job interviews and appointments, it's also okay to be on time. Just don't arrive late! First impressions count!

1. Pair work

Take turns reading these passages with a partner.

2. Group work

Ask two classmates what they think about arriving late to a party, an appointment and a job interview. When is it acceptable to arrive late? Discuss this with the class.

NOTES:

Unit 9

Five Years from Now

Unit 09 Five Years from Now

Conversation

- Talk about educational experiences
- Talk about personal qualities and characteristics
- Talk about career and life goals

Situations

- Search for a job
- Communicate work preferences
- Communicate work experience
- Learn job interview skills

Vocabulary Preview

Interview	Resume	Professional	Experience
Hobbies	Goals	Preference	Day care
Health care	Dental care	Vacation	Paid leave
Maternity leave	Fringe benefits	Manager	Office worker
Physical therapist	Radiologist technician	Dentist	Doctor
Accountant	Engineer	Editor	Optometrist

Let's Get Started

1. Review this list of vocabulary words. Translate the English words into Korean.

English	Korean	English	Korean
interview		fringe benefits	
resume		manager	
professional experience		office worker	
hobbies		optometrist	
goals		physical therapist	
preference		radiologist technician	
day care		dentist	
health / dental care		accountant	
paid leave		engineer	
maternity leave		editor	

NOTES:

2. Match the questions with the answers.

1) Where will you have the interview?	a. We offer childcare for employees.
2) Do you have any professional experience?	b. They make less than a doctor.
3) Does your company offer day care?	c. I want to be an engineer.
4) How much paid leave does she get?	d. It will be in the main office.
5) Do you want to be the manager?	e. Yes, I have three years of experience.
6) Are you studying to be an editor?	f. No, I prefer to be an office worker.
7) What is your preference for a career?	g. No, I'm studying to be an optometrist.
8) How much money does an accountant make?	h. She gets three weeks.

3. Pair Work. Use the questions and answers in part 2 to interview your partner.

4. What have you done? Place a check (✔) in the box if you have done the activity. After you complete the chart, ask two classmates what they have done.

What have you done?

Have you ever...	You	Classmate 1	Classmate 2
been on an interview?			
created an English resume?			
made a career goal?			
had a part-time job?			
been sent to day care as a child?			
enjoyed fringe benefits at work / school?			
enjoyed a hobby?			

5. What kind of person are you? Write about yourself, your characteristics and your personal qualities. Use the words from the box to help you.

Personal Qualities and Characteristics

Adjectives

outgoing	diligent	decisive	liberal
bubbly	lazy	organized	unconventional
positive	reliable	creative	conscientious
shy	kind	funny / humorous	traditional
introverted	friendly	dynamic	stubborn
hardworking	independent	conservative	determined

Say It Right

1. Listen to Madison interview Scott for a job. Follow along with the questions and write in the answer to each question in the blank provided. Audio

   1) What subjects do you get the best grades in?

   ____

   2) What subjects do you get the worst grades in?

   ____

   3) Do you have any work experience?

   ____

   4) What are two of your best personal qualities?

   ____

   5) What is your worst personal quality?

   ____

   6) How would you feel about working far away from your hometown?

   ____

   7) What are your career goals for the next 5 years?

   ____

2. Pair work

   Ask the interview questions from part 1 to your partner. Have your partner provide his or her own answer. Then, have your partner ask you the interview questions.

Speaking

Listen to the conversation between Joo Han and Janet. Answer the following questions. Audio

Joo Han : Thank you for coming here today.

Janet : It's my pleasure. Thank you for inviting me.

Joo Han : I'd like to start by asking if you have any previous professional experience in radiology.

Janet : As a matter of fact, I do. I worked at Willamette Falls Hospital in Oregon City for three years.

Joo Han : Wow, that's great. What did you find most challenging about that job?

Janet : Well, the hospital didn't offer maternity leave, so I won't be able to stay home with my new baby.

Joo Han : That's too bad. You'll be happy to hear that we offer 100 days of paid leave.

Janet : That sounds perfect. It's just what I need.

Joo Han : Next, I would like to know what your schedule preferences are.

Janet : I prefer to work Monday through Friday during the day. I would like to spend the evening at home with my husband.

Joo Han : Of course. And how would you feel about working at our remote clinic?

Janet : Ummm. . . I don't think I can. I don't have a car, and the bus doesn't go there. Will that be a problem?

Joo Han : Of course not. You are a highly qualified candidate. I would like to hire you anyway.

Janet : Oh, this is wonderful. When can I start?

1. What is happening?

2. Pair work

Practice the conversation with a partner.

3. Answer True or False for the statements about the conversation.

1) Joo Han wants a job at a hospital.	T	F
2) Janet is interviewing Joo Han.	T	F
3) Janet is pregnant.	T	F
4) Janet is interested in dental care.	T	F
5) Janet is a radiologist technician.	T	F
6) Joo Han wants Janet to work at a remote clinic.	T	F
7) Janet is single.	T	F
8) Joo Han offered Janet 100 days of paid leave.	T	F
9) Janet accepted a job with Joo Han.	T	F
10) Janet worked at a hospital for four years.	T	F

4. Answer the following questions about the conversation.

1) Where did Janet work before her interview with Joo Han?

____

2) Why did Janet leave her former job?

____

3) Why will Janet be happy with Joo Han and his job offer?

____

4) What is Janet's work schedule preference?

____

Listening Comprehension

Listen to this short story. Listen for the main idea and details. Audio

In many families today, both the mother and the father have jobs outside of the home. This can make it difficult to take care of the children. To help, some companies are changing the work rules. These companies are trying to be more family friendly. What are companies doing to become family friendly? Many companies are allowing their employees to work flexible hours. With flexible hours, or flextime, people can work full time, but they don't have to work a 9-5 schedule. Some employees choose to come in early and leave early. Some employees choose to work 10 hours one day and six hours the next. Most companies say that flexible hours increase productivity. In the United States, about one-third of full-time employees have flexible work schedules.

Family-friendly companies also allow two employees to share one job. Each employee does half of the job and gets half of the salary. In the United States, 27% of companies offer some kind of job sharing. Many family-friendly companies also give paid leave to both parents when a baby is born. In many countries, employers have to give female workers time off before and after the birth of a child. In the United States, for example, female employees get 12 weeks of unpaid time off. New mothers can stay at home, but they don't get their salary. In some countries, employers have to give all workers paid leave for the birth of a child. In Finland, for example, both male and female employees get paid leave. Women get 105 days of paid leave and men get 42!

The way people work is changing. For many people, that is a good thing.

1. Which title best fits the story? Circle your answer.

   1) Fringe-Benefit Companies

   2) Family Friendly Companies

   3) Flex-Hour Companies

2. Read the story out loud to your partner. Practice slowly and focus on your accent and pronunciation.

3. Answer the questions about the story.

   1) What are flexible work hours?

   2) What is job sharing?

   3) Why are some companies becoming more family friendly?

   4) Why do employees like flexible work hours?

   5) Why do employers like flexible work hours?

4. Fill in the blanks with the correct word. The sentences are from the text.

   1) Many companies are __________ their employees to work __________ hours.

   2) Most companies say that flexible hours __________ productivity.

   3) Family-friendly companies also allow two employees to __________ one job.

   4) To help, some companies are changing the work __________.

   5) With flexible hours, people can work __________, but they don't have to work a 9 to 5 __________.

   6) In many countries, employers have to give __________ workers

__________ before and after the birth of a child.

7) In Finland, for example, both __________ and female employees get paid leave.

8) In the United States, for example, female employees get 12 weeks of __________ time off.

9) Some employees __________ to come in early and leave early.

10) In some countries, employers have to give all workers paid __________ for the birth of a child.

NOTES:

Food for Thought

1. Review these idiomatic expressions. What do you think they mean?

1) Happy camper

2) Have it made

3) To brown nose

4) Throw in the towel

5) To put one's best foot forward

6) Crème de la crème

2. Pair work

Discuss your thoughts about the definitions with a partner.

3. Match the expressions with the meanings.

1) ____ Throw in the towel	a. To be very satisfied
2) ____ Be a happy camper	b. Start something well, or give a good first impression
3) ____ To brown nose	c. To say many kind but insincere things to a boss to gain favor
4) ____ To put one's best foot forward	d. To have an ideal or perfect situation
5) ____ Have it made	e. The best
6) ____ Crème de la crème	f. To quit

What in the World?

Audio

Resume styles are different in each country. Listen to Dawn and Tim talk about resume styles in the United States and Korea.

In the United States, it's important to show your skills, knowledge and abilities on your resume. It's best to begin the document with your name, contact information, including your e-mail address and phone number. Next, provide your educational experience. Then, you can continue with any professional experience and certifications you might have. In the United States you never include your age, weight, religion, height, or information about your family. It's illegal for potential employers to ask questions about these topics.

Resumes in Korea are not the same as in the United States. While people also include their names, contact information and educational experience, they include other information, too. For example, they often include a photo of themselves. Many times, grades are included with educational information. Employers might ask for religious, family or other personal information. It's acceptable to include your height, weight, age, and personal interests, too.

1. Pair work

Take turns reading these passages with a partner.

2. Group work

Ask two classmates their opinion of resume styles in Korea and the US. Is one style better than the other? Discuss this with the class.

Unit 10

Anything is Possible

Unit 10 Anything is Possible

Conversation

- Talk about choices and decisions
- Express opinions, likes and dislikes
- Talk about social issues
- Debate social issues

Situations

- Communicate choices
- Debate with friends
- Talk about important social topics

Vocabulary Preview

Hydroelectricity	Nuclear energy	Equity	Equality
Equal opportunity	Euthanasia	Sexism	Racism
Xenophobia	Unemployment	Demonstrations	Social security
Biodegradable	Conservation	Deforestation	Disposable
Ecosystem		Endangered species	
Environmental protection		Animal / human rights	

Let's Get Started

1. Review this list of vocabulary words. Translate the English words into Korean

▶ English	▶▶ Korean	▶ English	▶▶ Korean
hydroelectricity		xenophobia	
endangered species		unemployment	
animal / human rights		demonstrations	
equity		social security	
equality		environmental protection	
sexism		biodegradable	
equal opportunity		conservation	
nuclear energy		deforestation	
racism		disposable	
euthanasia		ecosystem	

2. Answer the following questions with the vocabulary words from part 1.

1) What do you call it when there isn't equal treatment between men and women?

2) What is it called when people cut down all the trees?

3) How can you protect the environment?

4) What do you call it when an animal is almost totally gone from earth?

5) What is it called when the same chances are given to all people?

3. Pair Work. Use the questions and answers in part 2 to interview your partner.

4. Classify the issues. Write each social issue or topic under the correct category. Issues may fit under more than one category.

Animal rights	Equity	Equality	Equal opportunity
Sexism	Racism	Xenophobia	Unemployment
Demonstrations	Social security	Nuclear energy	Disposable
Biodegradable	Conservation	Deforestation	Hydroelectricity
Ecosystem	Euthanasia	Endangered species	
Human rights	Environmental protection		

Humans/ Animals

The Environment

Energy

Public Issues

Say It Right

1. Listen to the following questions about social issues. Notice the stress and intonation of each question. Audio

   1) What do you think of euthanasia?

   2) How do you feel about human rights?

   3) What's your opinion on animal rights?

   4) Did you hear the latest news on environmental protection?

   5) What do you think of deforestation?

2. Listen again. This time, underline the words in each sentence that are emphasized. Do these questions have rising or falling intonation? Audio

3. Write three more questions about social issues.

   1)

   2)

   3)

Talking about the Issues	Asking about the Issues
In my opinion...	What's your opinion on...?
I think that...	What do you think about...?
I believe that...	Do you believe that...?
I heard that...	Did you hear that...?
I feel that...	How do you feel about...?
I like...	Do you like...?
I dislike...	Do you dislike...?

Speaking

Listen to the conversation between Sunny and Kristi. Answer the following questions. Audio

Sunn : Hey, Kristi, what do you think about sexism?

Kristi : I think it is complicated. Many people don't understand it well.

Sunny : I agree. My professor asked me today what I thought. I didn't have an answer. So, tell me, what do you think?

Kristi : I think it is a form of discrimination. It's unfair, in the 21st century, for men and women to be treated differently.

Sunn : Really? But aren't we different?

Kristi : Yes, Sunny, we are different, but our contributions to society are equally important. Men are not more important than women and women are not more important than men.

Sunn : I see. So, men and women are different, but equal?

Kristi : That's it. But if a man and a woman have the same job, then they should receive the same salary.

Sunn : So sexism isn't just about thinking men are better than women?

Kristi : No, it's also about equal opportunity in the work place.

Sunn : I think I'm beginning to understand this issue a lot better.

Kristi : I hope I helped. Like I said before, it's complicated.

Sunn : Yes, it is, but so are racism, deforestation and human rights.

Kristi : Isn't life wonderful?

1. What issue is being discussed?

2. Pair work

Practice the conversation with a partner.

3. Answer True or False for the statements about the conversation

1)	Sunny wants to understand racism.	T	F
2)	Sunny's professor asked her about sexism.	T	F
3)	Kristi thinks sexism is complicated.	T	F
4)	Men and women are different but equal.	T	F
5)	Sexism is a positive thing.	T	F
6)	Kristi should ask her professor about sexism.	T	F
7)	Sunny is more confused than before about sexism.	T	F
8)	Kristi said sexism is a form of discrimination.	T	F
9)	Sunny understands more about sexism now.	T	F
10)	Deforestation is also complicated.	T	F

NOTES:

4. Fill in the missing words from the conversation.

Sunny : Hey, Kristi, what do you (1) _______ (2) _______ sexism?

Kristi : I think it is (3) ________. Many people don't understand it well.

Sunny : I (4) ______. My professor (5) ______ me today what I thought. I didn't have an answer. So, tell me, what do you think?

Kristi : I think it is a form of (6) _________. It's unfair, in the 21st century, for men and women to be (7) ________ (8) _________ .

Sunny : Really? But aren't we different?

Kristi : Yes, Sunny, we are different, but our (9) ____________to society are equally important. Men are not more important than women and women are not more important than men.

Sunny : I see. So, men and women are different, but (10) __________?

Kristi : That's it. But if a man and a woman have the same job, then they (11) ________ (12) ___________the same salary.

NOTES:

Listening Comprehension

Listen to this short story. Listen for the main idea and details. Audio

Have you ever entered a tropical rainforest? It's a special, dark place completely different from anywhere else. It's a place where trees grow very tall. It is hot and humid in a rainforest. It rains a lot in the rainforest, but sometimes you don't know it's raining. The trees grow so closely together that the rain doesn't always reach the ground.

Rainforests make up only a small part of the earth's surface, about six percent. They are found in the tropical parts of the world. The largest rainforest in the world is the Amazon in South America. The Amazon covers over 1.2 billion acres, or almost five million square kilometers. The second largest rainforest is in Western Africa. There are also rainforests in Central America, Southeast Asia, Northeastern Australia and the Pacific Islands.

Rainforests provide us with many things. In fact, the Amazon Rainforest is called the "lungs of our planet" because it produces 20 percent of the world's oxygen. One-fifth of the world's fresh water is also found in the Amazon. Furthermore, one-half of the world's species of animals, plants, and insects live in the earth's rainforests. Eighty percent of the food we eat grows in the rainforest. For example, pineapples, bananas, tomatoes, corn, potatoes, chocolate, coffee and sugar all came from the rainforest. Twenty-five percent of the drugs we take when we're sick are made from plants that grow only in rainforests.

With all of the things we get from rainforests, it's surprising to find that we are destroying our rainforests. In fact, 1.5 acres, or 6,000 square meters, of rainforest disappear every second. The forests are being cut down to make fields for cows, to harvest plants and to clear land for farms. Along with losing countless valuable species, the destruction and deforestation in rainforests creates many problems worldwide. Destruction of rainforests leads to more pollution, less rain and less oxygen for the world.

1. Which title best fits the story? Circle your answer.

   1) Out of Rainforests
   2) Cut-Down Rainforests
   3) The Amazon is Big

2. Read the story out loud to your partner. Practice slowly and focus on your accent and pronunciation.

3. Answer the questions about the story.

   1) What valuable things come from the rainforest?
   2) Where in the world can rainforests be found?
   3) What is happening to rainforests?
   4) What percent of the earth's surface is covered in rainforests?
   5) Why is the destruction of rainforests bad?

4. In your opinion

   Answer the following questions using your feelings, thoughts and ideas.

   1) Would you like to visit a rainforest? Why or why not?
   2) What can the government do to protect rainforests?
   3) What can you do personally to protect rainforests?

5. Pair work

Ask these questions to your partner. Share your own answers with your partner.

6. What is the main idea of this reading? Circle the correct answer.

1) Kinds of forests
2) Where rainforests are located
3) Facts about rainforests
4) What food comes from rainforests

NOTES:

Food for Thought

1. Review these idiomatic expressions. What do you think they mean?

   1) Seize the day
   2) In your dreams
   3) Chicken scratch
   4) When it rains, it pours
   5) Raining cats and dogs
   6) Live wire

2. Pair work

   Discuss your thoughts about the definitions with a partner.

3. Match the expressions with the meanings.

1) In your dreams	a. Many bad things happen at one time
2) Raining cats and dogs	b. Very bad handwriting
3) Chicken scratch	c. Take advantage of a good opportunity
4) When it rains, it pours	d. An exciting or dynamic person
5) Live wire	e. Rain very hard
6) Seize the day	f. It will never happen

4. Group work

   Do you have similar idioms or expressions in your own language? Brainstorm in groups of three to four, about expressions of speech you use in your native language. Share your list with the class.

What in the World?

Important social issues change with time. Listen to the recording about social issues from the 1950's and 1960's. Audio

The 1950's - Cuban Revolution

The overthrow of Fulgencio Batista by Fidel Castro, Che Guevara and other forces in 1959 resulted in the creation of the first communist government in the Americas. The revolution marked the end of Cuban alignment with the Western world and began its association with the Eastern world, especially the Soviet Union.

The 1960's - American Civil Rights

Much of the political movements, and the people participating in them, came from the Civil Rights struggle in the South in the late 1950's and early 1960's. Black Americans began to challenge segregation in the South through various means, such as: boycotts, freedom rides, sit-ins, lawsuits and registering Blacks to vote.

1. Pair work

Take turns reading these passages with a partner.

2. Group work

As a class, discuss the social and political movements in Korea during the 1980's, 1990's and the first few years of the 21st century.

Unit 11

Happy Trails

Go Native!
Conversation
for English Language Learners

Unit 11 Happy Trails

Conversation

- Talk about travel destinations
- Talk about documents for travel
- Compare and contrast locations

Situations

- Make travel arrangements
- Talk about vacations
- Navigate international airports

Vocabulary Preview

Holiday	Passport	Visa	Travelers insurance
Tropical	Romantic	Adventure	Lazy
Travel agent	Reservation	Stand-by	Customs
Immigration	Declare (customs)	Toiletries	Vaccinations
Scenery	Embassy	Reception (hotel)	

Let's Get Started

1. Review this list of vocabulary words. Translate the English words into Korean.

▶ English	▶▶ Korean	▶ English	▶▶ Korean
holiday		reservation	
cruise		stand-by	
passport		customs	
visa		immigration	
travelers insurance		declare (customs)	
tropical		toiletries	
romantic		vaccinations	
adventure		scenery	
lazy		embassy	
travel agent		reception (hotel)	

NOTES:

2. Answer the following questions with the vocabulary words from part 1.

1) What is the name of the document that gives people permission to enter a country?

2) What is the name of the document that provides proof of nationality and identification?

3) Where can a traveler get help if they lose their passport while on holiday?

4) What is the name of the document that provides coverage in case of an emergency?

3. Pair Work. Use the questions and answers in part 2 to interview your partner.

4. Common travel phrases. Match the two columns to make common travel phrases.

1) Declare ...	a. a travel agent
2) Register ...	b. travelers insurance
3) Buy ...	c. a cruise / holiday
4) Fly ...	d. at the embassy
5) Take ...	e. stand-by
6) Call ...	f. it at customs

5. Pair work

Use the expressions of necessity and obligation from the box to ask and answer questions using the common travel phrases from part 4.

Example I should call the travel agent.

Expressions of Necessity

Statements	Questions
I / you should ...	Should I / you ...?
I / you must ...	Do I have to / you ...?
I / you ought to ...	Do I need to / you ...?
I / you need to ...	Can you tell me ...?
It's a good idea to ...	Do you know how ...?
I / you can ...	Can I / you ...?

NOTES:

Say It Right

1. Listen to the following statements related to travel. Notice the intonation and emphasis of each sentence. Audio

   1) I should make a reservation at the travel agency this week.

   2) Oh no! I forgot to process my visa.

   3) I would love to take a romantic holiday.

   4) After I went through immigration, I had to declare my souvenirs at customs.

2. Listen again. This time, underline the words in each sentence that are emphasized.

3. Write three statements using the expressions of like / dislike and verbs with the place names from the box below.

   Example I would love to travel to Ghana.

   1)

   2)

   3)

Expressions of desire	Verbs	Place Names
I would love	to visit	China
I never want	to see	Canada
I would hate	to travel	Thailand
I heard that	to live	Ghana
I feel that	to vacation in	Iceland
I like		Spain
I dislike		Greece

Speaking

Listen to the conversation between Andy and Wayne. Answer the following questions. Audio

Andy : I'm so excited about our holiday. I can hardly wait! Just think of all the beautiful scenery that awaits us. Europe, here we come!

Wayne : We just have to take care of a few details before we go.

Andy : What's left? We called the travel agency and bought travelers insurance. We also processed the visas and checked our passports and got our vaccines....

Wayne : I think we should confirm our reservations with reception at the hotel in Spain, first. It would be nice to know we have a place to sleep when we arrive.

Andy : I already did that.

Wayne : Really? Great. Looks like we are ready, after all.

Andy : So, when we arrive, what will happen at the airport? This is my first time traveling abroad, you know.

Wayne : Yes, I had forgotten. Well, first you will go through immigration. The agent will check your visa and passport.

Andy : Ok. Then what?

Wayne : Next, we collect our luggage and go through customs.

Andy : So immigration is where they process me, and customs is where they process my belongings?

Wayne : Yep. That's right. Just don't make any jokes about illegal or prohibited items. They won't think it's funny.

Andy : Fine. I'll save the jokes until after we leave the airport.

Wayne : Better yet, save them for the pretty European girls!

1. Where are they going?

2. Pair work

Practice the conversation with a partner.

3. Answer True or False for the statements about the conversation.

1) Wayne and Andy are going on vacation.	T	F
2) Andy has not confirmed the hotel reservation.	T	F
3) They will visit Germany.	T	F
4) Wayne has never traveled abroad before.	T	F
5) Immigration is where the passport is processed.	T	F
6) Customs is where the passport is processed.	T	F
7) Andy and Wayne want to meet girls in Spain.	T	F
8) You get your luggage before you go to customs.	T	F
9) Andy and Wayne still need their vaccinations.	T	F
10) They do not have travelers insurance.	T	F

4. Answer the following questions about the conversation.

1) Where will Andy and Wayne go on vacation?
2) What preparations have they made for their trip?
3) What happens at the airport?
4) What does Wayne say about illegal or prohibited items?
5) Who will Andy save his jokes for?

Listening Comprehension

Listen to this short story. Listen for the main idea and details. Audio

In Tokyo, it's an envelope with $850,000 in cash. At Florida's Disney World, it's a glass eye. At a hotel in England, it's a goat and a false leg. How are all of these things similar? They are unusual things that people have left in hotel rooms, airports, and on city streets.

Trish Martino works in the Lost and Found Center at an airport in a US city. "Sure, we find the usual stuff – cell phones, keys, sunglasses and wallets," she says, "But people also forget some weird things at the airport, too." What does Mrs. Martino find? For example, she's found a woman's false teeth in the bathroom and a mannequin in an airport waiting area. "How do you forget those things?" Martino wonders.

Nobuo Hasuda works for the Lost and Found Center in downtown Tokyo. The Center has almost 800,000 items. Three hundred thousand (300,000) of them are umbrellas! There are also many other things – jewelry and briefcases, snowshoes and musical instruments.

Mr. Hasuda keeps the lost and found items for six months and two weeks. After this time, the finder can take the item. This is good luck for some people. Remember the $850,000? The owner didn't claim it. Now, the money belongs to the finder!

1. Which title best fits the story? Circle your answer.

1) A Glass Eye Lost but Found

2) Lost and Found

3) People Lose their Minds on Vacation

2. Read the story out loud to your partner. Practice slowly and focus on your accent and pronunciation.

3. Answer the questions about the story.

1) What was found in England?

2) Who works at the Lost and Found Center in Tokyo?

3) What happens after six months and two weeks?

4) Where was a glass eye found?

5) How many umbrellas are at the Lost and Found Center in Tokyo?

4. In your opinion

Answer the following questions using your feelings, thoughts and ideas.

1) Would you turn in something you found in a hotel room or airport?

2) Have you ever lost anything? If yes, what was it and where did you lose it?

3) How would you feel if you lost your cell phone and all of its data?

5. Pair work

Ask these questions to your partner. Share your own answers with your partner.

6. Imagine you find $ 850,000. What are you going to do?

Food for Thought

1. Review these idiomatic expressions. What do you think they mean?

   1) When in Rome, do as the Romans do
   2) Rough it
   3) Fly by the seat of your pants
   4) Be in a pickle
   5) Cry over spilt milk
   6) Eat it up

2. Pair work

   Discuss your thoughts about the definitions with a partner.

3. Match the expressions with the meanings.

1) Fly by the seat of your pants	a. Stay in poor quality lodgings and have no luxuries
2) When in Rome, do as the Romans do	b. Be upset over something trivial
3) Be in a pickle	c. Have a difficult situation
4) Rough it	d. Enjoy something immensely
5) Eat it up	e. Be spontaneous
6) Cry over spilt milk	f. Follow local customs

4. Group work

   Do you have similar idioms or expressions in your own language? Brainstorm in groups of three to four, about expressions of speech you use in your native language. Share your list with the class.

What in the World?

Do you know your countries and continents? Label each continent and name three countries located there. * One continent has no official countries.

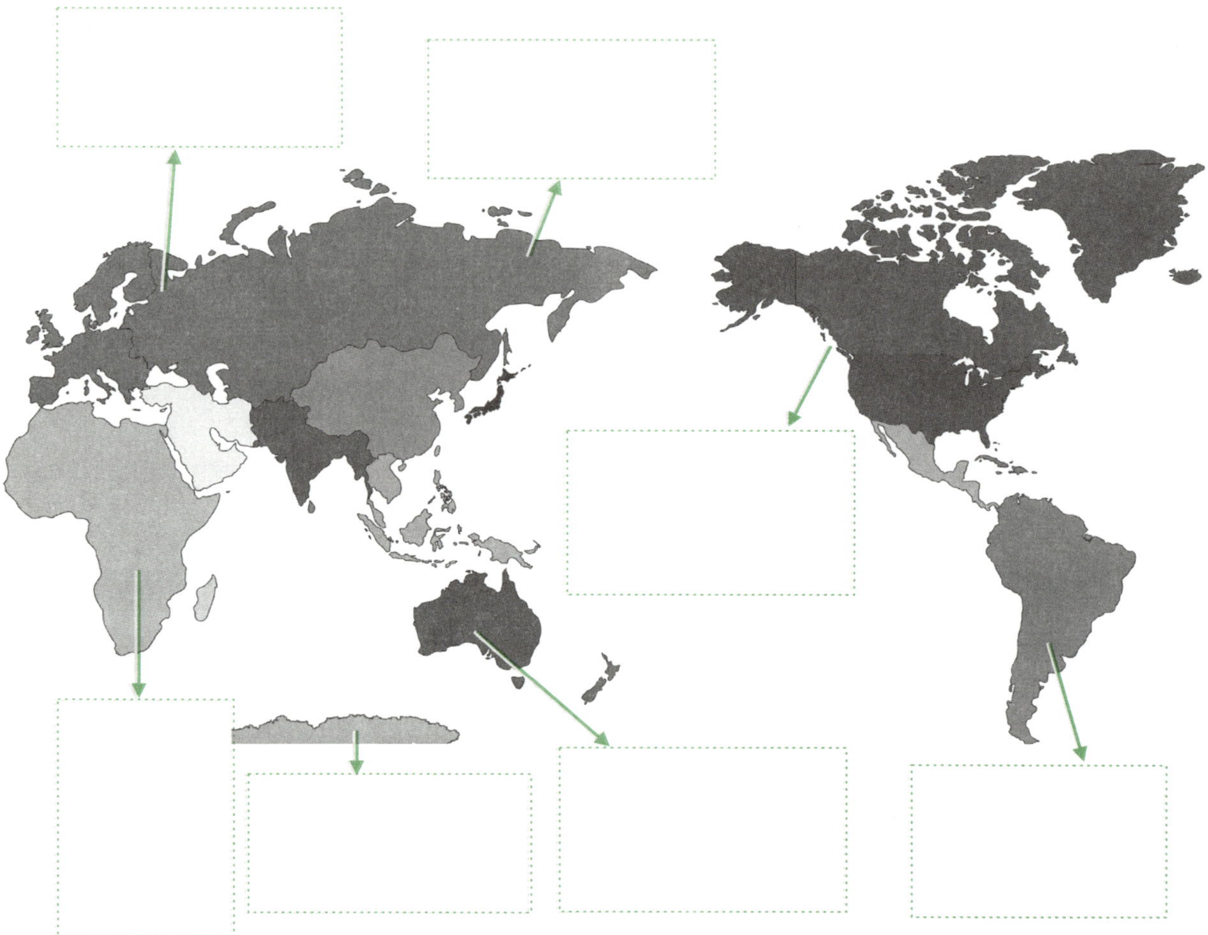

Unit 12

Wonderful World

Go Native!
Conversation
for English Language Learners

Unit 12 Wonderful World

Conversation

- Talk about facts and trivia
- Express expectations
- Talk about obligations

Situations

- Discuss world facts and trivia
- Communicate global socio-political dynamics
- Understand body language

Vocabulary Preview

Opinion	Fact	Trivia	Obligation
Expectation	Global	Silk	Steel
Brass	Ceramic	Handmade	Cotton
Organic	Leather	Metal	Valley
Summit	Sail	Cathedral	Factory
Import	Export		

Let's Get Started

1. Review this list of vocabulary words. Translate the English words into Korean.

▶ English	▶▶ Korean	▶ English	▶▶ Korean
opinion		handmade	
fact		organic	
trivia		leather	
obligation		metal	
expectation		valley	
global		summit	
silk		sail	
steel		cathedral	
brass		import	
cotton		export	

2. Fill in the following blanks with the vocabulary words from part 1.

1) When did you ____________ a mountain peak?

2) I like to _____________ a boat on a river.

3) _____________ can be classified as 'organic'.

4) ____________ is another word for 'a truth'.

5) _____________ is another word for 'personal thoughts'.

3. Pair Work. Use the information in part 2 to practice with your partner.

4. Match the vocabulary words with synonyms.

1) Valley	a. Send abroad
2) Expectation	b. Gorge
3) Global	c. Responsibility
4) Import	d. Place of worship
5) Export	e. Details, finer points
6) Cathedral	f. Worldwide
7) Trivia	g. Anticipation
8) Obligation	h. Introduce

5. What do you think of . . .? Write three related words for each vocabulary word.

1) Fact
2) Opinion
3) Cotton
4) Silk
5) Handmade

6. Pair work

Share your related vocabulary from part 5 with your partner. How are your answers similar? How are they different?

Say It Right

1. Listen to the following questions and statements about global trivia. Notice the stress and intonation of each statement. The italicized words should be stressed for more natural emphasis. Audio

❶ *Did you know* that there are *more* sheep in New Zealand than there are people?

❷ *Did you know* that the US imports *most* of its oil from *Canada*, and not the *Middle East*?

❸ *Did you know* that the majority of the world's population has never *made or received a phone call*?

❹ *Did you know* that the majority of the world's population *lives* on *less* than *$1 US a day*?

2. Listen to the conversation between Elaine and Byung Soo. Underline the words that are emphasized. Audio

Elaine : I need to bring some cheese to the party. Which one should I buy?

Byung Soo : You ought to buy the French cheese. It's the best.

Elaine : These are the options for importing cotton. What do you think about them?

Byung Soo : I am not happy with them.

3. Pair work

Practice each statement from part 3 with your partner.

Speaking

Listen to the conversation between Annika and Jae Ho. Answer the following questions. Audio

Annika : Hey, Jae Ho, how much world trivia do you know?

Jae Ho : Enough. I think I know more than you!

Annika : Really? Let's find out. Are you ready? Question one: how high is the summit of Mt. Everest?

Jae Ho : 29,002 feet or 8,840 meters. Question two?

Annika : Okay, which river is the world's longest?

Jae Ho : Yes, that would be the Nile, which flows through 10 African countries. You could sail from Egypt to the Democratic Republic of Congo, if you wanted. But the Amazon has much more water, so don't ask me which one is bigger. That's a different question.

Annika : So, you aren't that bad. Let's see if you can get this one!

Jae Ho : <u>Hit me with your best shot</u>!

Annika : Which country exports more steel than any other country in the world?

Jae Ho : That's easy; Japan.

Annika : Ahah! Think again! Did you know, in 2007, China surpassed Japan and Russia to become the world's leading steel exporter? China even exports more than the EU25.

Jae Ho : Ok, <u>you got me</u>, but how much do you really know? Can you tell me which country exports the most cotton?

Annika : Sure, that would be the United States of America exporting nearly 48% of the global cotton crops to the rest of the world. Were you aware that Australia wasn't even a close second?

Jae Ho : Ok, I didn't even know that. I give up. Game over. Do you want to get some coffee? Hey! Do you know where coffee came from?

1. What facts and trivia can you learn?

2. Pair work

Practice the conversation with a partner.

3. Answer True or False for the statements about the conversation.

1) The Nile is longer than the Amazon river.	T	F
2) Japan exports more steel than China.	T	F
3) China is the leading global importer of steel.	T	F
4) Australia exports more cotton than the US.	T	F
5) The Nile river flows through 10 countries.	T	F
6) The summit of Mt. Everest is 29,002 feet high.	T	F
7) Annika told Jae Ho the facts about China.	T	F
8) Annika asked Jae Ho if he wanted coffee.	T	F
9) Jae Ho challenges Annika in a trivia battle.	T	F
10) The US exports 45% of the global cotton crop.	T	F

4. Four phrases are underlined in the conversation. What do they mean? Write the answers below. Use context clues from the conversation for help.

   1) Hit me with your best shot :

   2) You got me :

   3) A close second :

   4) I give up. Game over :

5. Pair work

   Share your answers with your partner. Are your ideas similar?

6. Group work

   Discuss the phrases as a class. Ask your teacher what they mean.

NOTES:

Listening Comprehension

Listen to this short story. Listen for the main idea and details. Audio

Three skydivers made history over Mount Everest on October 5th by being the first people to parachute above the world's highest mountain. The parachutists, from New Zealand, Britain and Canada, trained for many years to make their jumps. Their plane flew about 150 meters above Everest's peak when they leapt out. They had to wear oxygen masks and parachutes that were larger than usual to help them in the thin air. The three were in freefall for 30 seconds before their chutes opened and they glided down to land. A member of the jumpers' support team Krishna Aryal explained to the Reuters news agency what the jumps looked like from the ground: "They looked like tiny birds flying in the blue sky as they jumped from the plane," he said.

The skydivers were over the moon with their jump over Everest. New Zealander Wendy Smith said: "It was stunning. I had never seen so many mountains before. To be on top of the world was simply stunning." Britain's Holly Budge agreed, saying her jump was "just spectacular". Their jumps broke several skydiving records. They entered the record books for making the highest skydiving freefall at nearly 8,900 meters. They also landed on the world's highest drop zone at 3,761 meters. Twenty-nine more daredevils are waiting for favorable weather conditions to make the same jump. The thrill seekers are part of the 'Everest Skydive 2008' event organized by the British extreme sports company High and Wild.

1. Which title best fits the story? Circle your answer.

   1) Historic Jumps Made Above Everest

   2) Parachutists Jump A Lot

   3) Parachutists Break Records and Legs Jumping from Everest

2. Read the story out loud to your partner. Practice slowly and focus on your accent and pronunciation.

3. Answer the questions about the story.

   1) What special items did the skydivers use because the air was thin?

   2) What did the jump look like from the ground?

   3) What did Wendy Smith think of the jump?

   4) Who organized this event?

4. Match the synonyms from the story.

5. Which of these places would you like to see most? Discuss your answers with your partner.

   1) Mt. Everest

   2) The Galapagos Islands

   3) Niagara Falls

   4) The Great Barrier Reef

   5) The Sahara Desert

   6) Antarctica

Food for Thought

1. Review these idiomatic expressions. What do you think they mean?

   1) It takes all kinds
   2) Life is like a box of chocolates
   3) On cloud nine
   4) Once in a blue moon
   5) A cloud on the horizon
   6) To be over the moon

2. Pair work

   Discuss your thoughts about the definitions with a partner.

3. Match the expressions with the meanings.

1) Life is like a box of chocolates	a. very excited
2) On cloud nine	b. you need all types of people
3) To be over the moon	c. anything is possible
4) Once in a blue moon	d. very happy or elated
5) A cloud on the horizon	e. hardly ever
6) It takes all kinds	f. bad news or a bad event is coming

What in the World?

No matter where you are in the world, you start each conversation with a non-verbal greeting. This is also known as body language. Audio

1. Listen to the following passages about body language in different countries.

❶ Crossing your arms in front of you, in the US, is a sign of closed communication.

❷ A 'thumbs up' sign in Costa Rica is asking for a ride. This is also known as 'hitch-hiking'.

❸ Pointing your finger to your eye tells others to watch out and be careful in South America.

❹ Staring at someone, in many Western countries, is considered rude.

❺ Americans will motion for you with an upward-facing finger, while Koreans use a downward-facing hand.

❻ Tapping your watch, or the area on your wrist where your watch would be, shows some-one that they are late.

2. Pair work

Take turns reading these passages with a partner.

3. Group work

Ask two classmates their opinion of body language cues in Korea. What are some of the common signs and cues used? Discuss this with the class.

NOTES:

Appendix

Glossary of Common Idiomatic Expressions

Go Native! Conversation for English Language Learners

Glossary of Common Idiomatic Expressions

A

A bit much

If something is excessive or annoying, it is a bit much.

A day late and a dollar short

(USA) If something is a day late and a dollar short, it is too little, too late.

A little bird told me

If someone doesn't want to say where they got some information from, they can say that a little bird told them.

A long row to hoe

Something that is a long row to hoe is a difficult task that takes a long time.

A penny for your thoughts

This idiom is used as a way of asking someone what they are thinking about.

A picture is worth a thousand words

A picture can often get a message across much better than the best verbal description.

A pretty penny

If something costs a pretty penny, it is very expensive.

A steal

If something is a steal, it costs much less than it is really worth.

Absence makes the heart grow fonder

This idiom means that when people are apart, their love grows stronger.

Accident waiting to happen

If something is an accident waiting to happen, there's definitely going to be an accident or it's bound to go wrong. ('Disaster waiting to happen' is also used.)

Across the board

If something applies to everybody, it applies across the board.

Across the pond

(UK) This idiom means on the other side of the Atlantic Ocean, used to refer to the US or the UK depending on the speaker's location.

Actions speak louder than words

This idiom means that what people actually do is more important than what they say- people can promise things but then fail to deliver.

Add fuel to the fire

If people add fuel to the fire, they make a bad situation worse.

Air your dirty laundry in public

If you air your dirty laundry in public, you reveal aspects of your private life that should really remain private, by telling a secret, arguing in public, etc.

B

Back to square one

If you are back to square one, you have to start from the beginning again.

Bad apple

A person who is bad and makes others bad is a bad apple.

Bad egg

A person who cannot be trusted is a bad egg. Good egg is the opposite.

Baker's dozen

A Baker's dozen is 13 rather than 12.

Ball is in your court

If the ball is in your court, it is up to you to make the next decision or step.

Ballpark figure

A ballpark figure is a rough or approximate number (guesstimate) to give a general idea of something, like a rough estimate for a cost, etc.

Bare your heart

If you bare your heart to someone, you tell him or her your personal and private feelings. ('Bare your soul' is an alternative form of the idiom.)

Barking up the wrong tree

If you are barking up the wrong tree, it means that you have completely misunderstood something or are totally wrong.

Barrel of laughs

If someone's a barrel of laughs, they are always joking and you find them funny.

Basket case

If something is a basket case, it is so bad that it cannot be helped.

Be all ears

If you are all ears, you are very eager to hear what someone has to say.

Bear fruit

If something bears fruit, it produces positive results.

Beat about the bush

If someone doesn't say clearly what they mean and tries to make it hard to understand, they are beating about (around) the bush.

Beauty is in the eye of the beholder

Beauty is in the eye of the beholder means that different people will find different things beautiful and that the differences of opinion don't matter greatly.

C

Calm before the storm

A calm time immediately before a period of violent activity or argument is the calm before the storm.

Cash cow

A product, business, etc, that generates a continuous flow of money or a high proportion of overall profits is a cash cow.

Cast iron stomach

A person with a cast iron stomach can eat or drink anything without any ill effects.

Cat got your tongue?

If someone asks if the cat has got your tongue, they want to know why you are not speaking when they think you should.

Change of heart

If you change the way you think or feel about something, you have a change of heart.

Chase rainbows

If someone chases rainbows, they try to do something that they will never achieve.

Cheat death

If someone cheats death, they narrowly avoid a major problem or accident.

Chip off the old block

If someone is a chip off the old block, they closely resemble one or both of the parents in character.

Clean slate

If you start something with a clean slate, then nothing bad from your past is taken into account.

Climb on the bandwagon

When people climb on the bandwagon they do something because it is popular and everyone else is doing it.

Coast is clear

When the coast is clear, the people supposed to be watching you are not there and you are able to move or leave.

Cold day in hell

This is used as a prediction there is no chance some event or condition will ever happen. 'There will be a cold day in hell before he manages it.'

Cold shoulder

If you give or show someone the cold shoulder, you are deliberately unfriendly and uncooperative towards him or her.

Come out of the woodwork

When things come out of the woodwork, they appear unexpectedly. ('Crawl out of the woodwork' is also used.)

Cutting edge

Something that is cutting edge is at the forefront of progress in its area.

D

Days are numbered

When someone's days are numbered, they are expected to die soon.

Dead air

When there is a period of total silence, there is dead air.

Dead wrong

If someone is dead wrong, they are absolutely in error, absolutely incorrect or of incorrect opinion.

Deep pockets

If someone has deep pockets, they are wealthy.

Devil's advocate

If someone plays devil's advocate in an argument, they adopt a position they don't believe in just for the sake of the argument.

Diamond in the rough

A diamond in the rough is someone or something that has great potential, but isn't refined and polished.

Different strokes for different folks

(USA) This idiom means that different people do things in different ways that suit them.

Dime a dozen

(USA) If something is a dime a dozen, it is extremely common, possibly too common.

Dirty dog

A dirty dog is an untrustworthy person.

Dog eat dog

In a dog eat dog world, there is intense competition and rivalry, where everybody thinks only of himself or herself.

Doggy bag

If you ask for a doggy bag in a restaurant, they will pack the food you haven't eaten for you to take home.

Don't bite the hand that feeds

When someone says this to you, they are trying to tell you not to act against those on whom you depend.

Don't catch your chickens before they're hatched

This means that you should wait until you know whether something has produced the results you desire, rather than acting beforehand. ('Don't count your chickens until they've hatched' is an alternative.)

Don't cry over spilt milk

When something bad happens and nothing can be done to help it people say, 'Don't cry over spilt milk'.

Don't sweat the small stuff

(USA) This is used to tell people not to worry about trivial or unimportant issues.

E

Eager beaver

A person who is extremely keen is an eager beaver.

Eagle eyes

Someone who has eagle eyes sees everything; no detail is too small.

Easy as ABC

Something that is as easy as ABC is very easy or simple.

Eat like a bird

If someone eats like a bird, they eat very little.

Eat like a horse

Someone who eats like a horse, eats a lot.

Eat like a pig

If someone eats like a pig, they either eat too much or they have bad table manners.

Elbowroom

If you haven't got enough elbowroom, you haven't got enough space.

Elephant in the room

An elephant in the room is a problem that everyone knows very well but no one talks about because it is taboo, embarrassing, etc.

Eleventh hour

If something happens at the eleventh hour, it happens right at the last minute.

Etched in stone

Something, especially rules and customs, that cannot be changed at all is said to be etched in stone.

Every dog has its day

This idiom means that everyone gets their moment to shine.

Every man and his dog

A lot of people - as in sending out invitations to a large number of people.

Eye-opener

Something surprising or unexpected which reveals the truth about something or someone.

F

Face only a mother could love

When someone has a face only a mother could love, they are ugly.

Face the music

If you have to face the music, you have to accept the negative consequences of something you have done wrong.

Free-for-all

A free-for-all is a fight or contest in which everyone gets involved and rules are not respected.

Frog in my throat

If you have a frog in your throat, you can't speak or you are losing your voice because you have a problem with your throat.

Full bore

If something is full bore, it involves the maximum effort or is complete and thorough.

Full circle

When something has come full circle, it has ended up where it started.

Full Monty

(UK) If something is the Full Monty, it is the real thing, not reduced in any way.

Full of beans

If someone's full of beans, they are very energetic.

Full of hot air

Someone who is full of hot air talks a lot of rubbish.

Full of oneself

Someone who acts in a arrogant or egotistical manner is full of himself/herself.

Full of piss and vinegar

Someone who's full of piss and vinegar is full of youthful energy.

Full swing

If a something is in full swing, it is going or doing well.

Full throttle

If you do something full throttle, you do it with as much speed and energy as you can.

Fur coat and no knickers

Someone with airs and graces, but no real class is fur coat and no knickers.

Fuzzy thinking

Thinking or ideas that do not agree with the facts or information available.

G

Get it off your chest

If you get something off your chest, you confess to something that has been troubling you.

Get my drift

If you get someone's drift, you understand what he or she is trying to say.

Get on your soapbox

If someone gets on their soapbox, they hold forth (talk a lot) about a subject they feel strongly about.

Get your goat

If something gets your goat, it annoys you.

Give someone the runaround

If someone gives you the runaround, they make excuses and give you false explanations to avoid doing something.

Go bananas

If you go bananas, you are wild with excitement, anxiety, or worry.

Go Dutch

If you go Dutch in a restaurant, you pay equal shares for the meal.

Go fly a kite

(USA) This is used to tell someone to go away and leave you alone.

Go play in traffic

This is used as a way of telling someone to go away.

Go round in circles

If people are going round in circles, they keep discussing the same thing without reaching any agreement or coming to a conclusion.

Golden touch

Someone with a golden touch can make money from or be successful at anything they do.

Gone fishing

If someone has gone fishing, they are not very aware of what is happening around them.

Grass roots

This idiom is often used in politics, where it refers to the ordinary people or voters. It can be used to mean people at the bottom of a hierarchy.

Grease monkey

A grease monkey is an idiomatic term for a mechanic.

Greek to me

If you don't understand something, it's all Greek to you.

H

Hair of the dog

If someone has a hair of the dog, they have an alcoholic drink as a way of getting rid of a hangover, (the unpleasant effects of having drunk too much alcohol the night before.) It is commonly used as a way of excusing having a drink early on in the day.

Happy medium

If you reach a happy medium, you are making a compromise, reaching a conclusion or decision.

Hard to come by

If something is hard to come by, it is difficult to find.

Have a ball

If you have a ball, you have a great time, a lot of fun.

Have a go

If you have a go, you try to do something, often when you don't think you have much chance of succeeding.

Have the guts

Someone who has enough courage to do something has the guts to do it.

Have your cake and eat it too

If someone wants to have their cake and eat it too, they want everything their way, especially when their wishes are contradictory.

Healthy as a horse

If you're as healthy as a horse, you're very healthy.

Hear a pin drop

If there is complete silence in a room, you can hear a pin drop.

Hear on the grapevine

To receive information indirectly through a series of third parties, similar to a rumor.

High and dry

If you are left high and dry, you are left alone and given no help at all when you need it.

Highway robbery

Something that is ridiculously expensive, especially when you have no choice but to pay, is a highway robbery.

Hit the books

If you hit the books, you study hard.

Hit the sack

When you hit the sack, you go to bed.

Hold your horses

If someone tells you to hold your horses, you are doing something too fast and they would like you to slow down.

I

Icing on the cake

This expression is used to refer to something good that happens on top of an already good thing or situation.

If Mohammed won't come to the mountain, the mountain must come to Mohammed

If something cannot or will not happen the easy way, then sometimes it must be done the hard way.

If you can't stand the heat, get out of the kitchen

Originally a Harry S. Truman quote, this means that if you can't take the pressure, then you should remove yourself from the situation.

If you'll pardon my French

This idiom is used as a way of apologizing for swearing.

In a flash

If something happens in a flash, it happens very quickly indeed.

In a tight spot

If you're in a tight spot, you're in a difficult situation.

In one ear and out the other

If something goes in one ear and out the other, you forget it as soon as you've heard it because it was too complicated, boring etc.

In over your head

If someone is in over their head, they are out of the depth in something they are involved in, and may end up in a mess.

In the doghouse

If someone is in the doghouse, they are in disgrace and very unpopular at the moment.

In the driver's seat

If you are in the driver's seat, you are in charge of something or in control of a situation.

It takes two to tango

This idiom is used to suggest that when things go wrong, both sides are involved and neither side is completely innocent.

J

Jane Doe

Jane Doe is a name given to an unidentified female who may be party to legal proceedings, or to an unidentified person in hospital, or dead. John Doe is the male equivalent.

John Doe

John Doe is a name given to an unidentified male who may be party to legal proceedings, or to an unidentified person in hospital, or dead. Jane Doe is the female equivalent.

Jump the gun

If you jump the gun, you start doing something before the appropriate time.

Jump through hoops

If you are prepared to jump through hoops for someone, you are prepared to make great efforts and sacrifices for them.

Jump to a conclusion

If someone jumps to a conclusion, they evaluate or judge something without a sufficient examination of the facts.

Just for the heck of it

When someone does something just for the heck of it, they do it without a good reason.

Just for the record

If something is said to be just for the record, the person is saying it so that people know but does not necessarily agree with or support it.

Just in the nick of time

If you do something just in the nick of time, you manage to do it just in time, with seconds to spare.

Just what the doctor ordered

If something's just what the doctor ordered, it is precisely what is needed.

K

Keep in touch

If you keep in touch with someone, you keep communicating with him or her even though you may live far apart.

Keep someone at arm's length

If you keep someone or something at arm's length, you keep a safe distance away from them.

Keep someone on his or her toes

If you keep someone on their toes, you make sure that they concentrate on what they are supposed to do.

Keep the wolf at bay

If you keep the wolf at bay, you make enough money to avoid going hungry or falling heavily into debt.

Keep up with the Joneses

People who try to keep up with the Joneses are competitive about material possessions and always try to have the latest and best things.

Keep your chin up

This expression is used to tell someone to have confidence.

Keep your cool

If you keep your cool, you don't get excessively excited or disturbed in a bad situation.

Keep your head above water

If you are just managing to survive financially, you are keeping your head above water.

Keep your nose clean

If someone is trying to keep their nose clean, they are trying to stay out of trouble by not getting involved in any sort of wrong-doing.

Kick a habit

If you kick a habit, you stop doing it.

Kill two birds with one stone

When you kill two birds with one stone, you resolve two difficulties or matters with a single action.

Kindred spirit

A kindred spirit is someone who feels and thinks the way you do.

King of the castle

The king of the castle is the person who is in charge of something or in a very comfortable position compared to their companions.

Knee-jerk reaction

A knee-jerk reaction is an instant, instinctive response to a situation.

Knock 'em dead

'Knock 'em dead' is used as a way of wishing someone luck before they give a performance or have to appear before people, as in an interview, etc. ('em = them)

L

Larger than life

If something is excessive or exaggerated, it is larger than life.

Last hurrah

If an elderly person does something special before they die, it is a last hurrah.

Last straw

The last straw is the final problem that makes someone lose their temper or the problem that finally brought about the collapse of something. It comes from an Arabic story, where a camel was loaded with straw until a single straw placed on the rest of the load broke its back.

Learn the ropes

If you are learning the ropes, you are learning how to do something.

Leave no stone unturned

If you look everywhere to find something, or try everything to achieve something, you leave no stone unturned.

Left-handed compliment

A left-handed compliment is one that sounds like praise but has an insulting meaning. ('Backhanded compliment' is an alternative form.)

Leopard can't change its spots

People cannot change basic aspects of their character, especially negative ones. ("A leopard doesn't change its spots" is also used.)

Lesser of two evils

Something that is the lesser of two evils is an unpleasant option, but not as bad as the other.

Let bygones be bygones

If people decide to let bygones be bygones, they decide to forget old problems or grievances they have with each other.

Let the cat out of the bag

If you accidentally reveal a secret, you let the cat out of the bag.

Let the chips fall where they may

This means that we shouldn't try to control events, because destiny controls them.

Let your guard down

If you let your guard down, you relax and stop looking out for danger.

Let your hair down

If someone lets their hair down, they relax and stop feeling inhibited or shy.

Light at the end of the tunnel

If you can see light at the end of the tunnel, then you can see some signs of hope in the future, though things are difficult at the moment.

Like a bat out of hell

This expression means extremely quickly.

M

Make a mint

If someone is making a mint, they are making a lot of money.

Make a monkey of someone

If you make a monkey of someone, you make him or her look foolish.

Make a mountain out of a molehill

If somebody makes a mountain out of a molehill, they exaggerate the importance or seriousness of a problem.

Make ends meet

If somebody finds it hard to make ends meet, they have problems living on the money they earn.

Make headway

If you make headway, you make progress.

Make out like a bandit

(USA) If someone is extremely successful in a venture, they make out like a bandit.

Make waves

If someone makes waves, they cause a lot of trouble.

Make your blood boil

If something makes your blood boil, it makes you very angry.

Make your flesh crawl

If something makes your flesh crawl, it really scares or revolts you. ('Make your flesh creep' is an alternative. 'Make your skin crawl' is also used.)

Man of his word

A man of his word is a person who does what he says and keeps his promises.

Monkey business

If children get up to monkey business, they are behaving naughtily or mischievously. This is the same as 'monkeying around'.

Monkey see, monkey do

This idiom means that children will learn their behavior by copying what they see happening around them.

More than one way to skin a cat

When people say that there is more than one way to skin a cat, they mean that there are different ways of achieving the same thing.

Music to my ears

If something someone says is music to your ears, it is exactly what you had wanted to hear.

My hands are tied

If your hands are tied, you are unable to act for some reason.

N

Nerves of steel

If someone has nerves of steel, they don't get frightened when other people do.

Nest egg

If you have some money saved for the future, it is a nest egg.

Ninth circle of hell

In Dante's Inferno, the ninth circle of hell is the centre where the worst punishments are found, so it is used idiomatically for something that couldn't get worse.

No laughing matter

Something that is no laughing matter is very serious.

No skin off my nose

If something's no skin off your nose, it doesn't affect or bother you at all.

No spring chicken

If someone is no spring chicken, they are not young.

No strings attached

If something has no strings attached, there are no obligations or requirements involved.

Not a snowball's chance in hell

There is absolutely no possibility of something happening if there's not a snowball's chance in hell.

Not all there

If someone isn't all there, they are a little bit stupid or crazy.

Nuts and bolts

The nuts and bolts are the most essential components of something.

O

On a roll

If you're on a roll, you're moving from success to success.

On a silver platter

If you hand or give something on a silver platter to someone, you let him or her have it too easily.

On all fours

If someone is on all fours, they crawl.

On the rebound

If someone is on the rebound, their relationship has recently ended and they are emotionally unstable.

On top of the world

If you are on top of the world, everything is going well for you.

P

Paint the town red

If you go for a night out with lots of fun and drinking, you paint the town red.

Pandora's box

If you open a Pandora's box, something you do causes all sorts of trouble that you hadn't anticipated.

Pass the buck

If you pass the buck, you avoid taking responsibility by saying that someone else is responsible.

Pay through the nose

If you pay through the nose for something, you pay a very high price for it.

Pen is mightier than the sword

The idiom 'the pen is mightier than the sword' means that words and communication are more powerful than wars and fighting.

Penny pincher

A penny pincher is a mean person or who is very frugal.

Pick up the tab

A person who pays for everyone picks up the tab.

Piece of cake

If something is a piece of cake, it is really easy.

Play the fool

If someone plays the fool, they behave in a silly way to make people laugh. ('Act the fool' is an alternative form.)

Play with fire

If people take foolish risks, they are playing with fire.

Pleased as punch

When someone is pleased as punch, they are very satisfied about something

Poetry in motion

Something that is poetry in motion is beautiful to watch.

Point the finger

When you point the finger at someone, you are accusing and blaming them for something.

Pot calling the kettle black

If someone hypocritically criticizes a person for something that they themselves do, then it is a case of the pot calling the kettle black.

Pull a rabbit out of your hat

If you pull a rabbit out of a hat, you do something that no one was expecting.

Q

Quick as a flash

If something happens quick as a flash, it happens very fast indeed.

Quick buck

If you make some money easily, you make a quick buck.

Quick fix

A quick fix is an easy solution, especially one that will not last.

Quiet as a mouse

If someone's as quiet as a mouse, they make absolutely no noise.

R

Rack your brain

If you rack your brain, you think very hard when trying to remember something. ('Rack your brains' is an alternative.)

Rags to riches

Someone who starts life very poor and becomes rich goes from rags to riches.

Rake someone over the coals

(USA) If you rake someone over the coals, you criticize or scold them severely.

Rank and file

The rank and file are the ordinary members of a company, organisation, etc, excluding the managers and directors.

Rat race

The rat race is the ruthless, competitive struggle for success in work, etc.

Raw deal

If you get a raw deal, you are treated unfairly.

Read between the lines

If you read between the lines, you find the real message in what you're reading or hearing; a meaning that is not available from a literal interpretation of the words.

Real trouper

A real trouper is someone who will fight for what they believe in and doesn't give up easily. (People often use 'Real trooper' as the two words sound the same.)

Recharge your batteries

If you recharge your batteries, you do something to regain your energy after working hard for a long time.

Recipe for disaster

A recipe for disaster is a mixture of people and events that could only possibly result in trouble.

Red carpet

If you give someone the red-carpet treatment, you give them a special welcome to show that you think they are important. You can roll out the red carpet, too.

Red letter day

A red letter day is one of good luck, when something special happens to you.

Red light district

The red light district is the area of a town or city where there is prostitution, sex shops, etc.

Right up my alley

If something is right up your alley, it suits you perfectly.

Rise and shine

If you wake up full of energy, you rise and shine.